Nicki Defago

First published in 2005 by Fusion Press,
a division of Satin Publications Ltd.
101 Southwark Street
London SE1 0JF
UK
info@visionpaperbacks.co.uk
www.visionpaperbacks.co.uk
Publisher: Sheena Dewan

A catalogue record for this book is available from the British Library.

ISBN: 1-904132-63-4

2 4 6 8 10 9 7 5 3

Cover and text design by ok?design
Printed and bound in the UK by Mackays of Chatham Ltd, Chatham, Kent

Author's Note

The author is not a member of any childfree organisation or a campaigner for the rights of childfree people.

CONTENTS

Preface

A while ago I met an old friend who I hadn't seen for 20 years.

'How's Mary-Anne?' she asked, after we'd caught up on our lives. Mary-Anne and I were teenage contemporaries and are still in touch.

'Fine,' I reported. 'She's married with four kids now!'

My friend shook her head with a look of grim sympathy. 'How ghastly,' she said, and I thought, here's someone I identify with.

Not having children seems an entirely logical decision, not only because of the wonderful lifestyle it allows, but because the world is so over-populated anyway. Yet after I was married and people asked when (rarely if) my husband Jim and I were going to start a family, reactions to our lack of intent were so extraordinary that they prompted the writing of this book.

Choosing to be childfree brings with it a fantastic sense of freedom for which I feel grateful every day. It would have been easy to 'follow the pack' because society so expects us to conform to tradition. But to have carefully considered the long-term implications of creating new lives and subsequently decided against is empowering. We've never looked back.

This book is not about whether people should or should not have children.

It is about personal choice.

it's wonderful when that's the case, but it's not and never has been the making of everyone. Parenthood is now a choice, though talking about it in such terms is only just becoming acceptable in a society still steeped in the values of the now outdated 'traditional family'.

When I got married to my husband Jim we didn't know if we wanted children. Hearing only favourable endorsements from everyone around made me suspicious, so I embarked on my own research – in my nearest Borders bookshop. The first thing I noticed was attitudes. When I asked at the counter, 'Have you got any books about women who don't want children?' the assistant looked taken aback. I felt rather embarrassed, as if I'd enquired after something inappropriate. After a puzzled exchange ('What do you ... *mean*?'), she waved me in the direction of 'Feminism', then 'Self-help'. There was nothing in either section, but ultimately I found for myself a couple of titles under 'Pregnancy and Childcare'. The irony wasn't lost, but in fact that was the best place for what I was looking for. Being uncertain about motherhood needn't automatically class you as a feminist, and it's a label many people feel uncomfortable with. Nor did I have a problem, just a decision to make, so the 'Skip Your Way to a Happier You' books weren't relevant either. First and foremost I was an average person considering life's options and my focus at the time was pregnancy and childcare – albeit with the subtext 'is it a good idea or not?'

In the UK, it's estimated that about a quarter of women in their thirties today won't have children by the time they're 45. It may be circumstantial – for fertility reasons or not meeting a suitable partner – but an estimated one in five women will actively decide that she doesn't want to become a mother. Australian figures are about the same and in New Zealand couples without children are expected to become the most common family type within the next few years. Ten per cent of the American population is childfree by choice and a recent survey showed seven per cent of Canadian women and eight per cent of Canadian men aged 20 to 34 have no intention of having children. The rise of adult-only families in Japan is significantly changing the country's cultural landscape.[1] After China, where the decision is enforced, Spain has the lowest birth rate in the world and the childfree notion is even impacting on family-orientated cultures like Greece.[2]

Sixty years ago in the UK about one in 11 women was childless at the age of 45, but there was no research into whether any made a conscious decision not to reproduce.[3] It was simply assumed that a married woman in possession of a good husband must be in want of a baby – a sentiment that hasn't changed over the years as much as one might suppose. There are no formal statistics relating to childless men.

In Borders there were rows upon rows of books detailing every possible eventuality for before, during and after pregnancy, but the few titles available for women who don't necessarily want children seemed either hallowed and weirdly lacking indefinite articles – *Will You Be Mother?*[4] and *Without Child*[5] – or rather clinical and alarming, *Childfree and Sterilized*[6] being a bit extreme for many. If you have or are about to have a baby, you're extremely well catered for in the reading department. Amazon offers more than a thousand titles on the single subject of what children eat, but if you're undecided about starting a family or resolutely childfree, you'll go hungry.

Outside the United States the word childfree is relatively new, but it's gaining popularity because it suggests something positive as opposed to child*less*. It's important to acknowledge the difference between those people who choose not to have children and those who are unable.

> Anyone who wishes to contribute to this debate should recognise that there is as large a difference between 'childfree' and 'childless' as there is between choosing to close your eyes and being born blind.
>
> *Martin, Dorchester*

For this book I've spoken to all sorts of people who don't have children for a variety of reasons. There's a prevalent assumption that motherhood is still every woman's favoured destiny, therefore many contributors are women like myself who are in a relationship and so 'well poised' to become mothers, but won't be doing so. Many contributors do have kids, but most agree that family life isn't the 'be all and end all' for everyone.

Opinions range from the glib:

> Don't say my name, but I just can't be arsed to have kids.

to the philosophical:

> Is parenthood an exercise in disillusion? When our own youth has gone and the hopes and ambitions we had for ourselves appear unreachable, is it then

> that we give up, get pregnant and hand on our dreams to someone else?

The childfree debate often gets polarised into whether people should or should not have children, but many of us living in affluent nations can choose any number of different paths in our lives and whether one opts for parenthood or being childfree is largely irrelevant. Arguing about it seems a ridiculous luxury given that such privilege is denied to most of the world's inhabitants. All that really matters is that individuals have the freedom to make the decision that's best for them. However, this is not always easy because having children is the expected, acceptable norm, whereas not having children is still considered odd or unusual in many circles. Promoting the validity of a childfree life is important, just as bringing a new life into the world is a serious business worthy of careful consideration.

> As a parent myself, it is a very courageous thing for someone not to have children. It's much harder, there is definitely a stigma. I had children at 38, my brother is childless by choice and I have friends who are childless, but not by choice. It is much easier to have a child on the stigma level, but it is so profoundly difficult to be a good parent that no one who doesn't want the challenge should feel they have to.
>
> *Sherman, UK*

We all arrange our lives in different ways. Jim and I love to travel and, though we work in London for most of the year, not being tied to a school timetable allows us to take a few months off over the winter. We both teach English as a foreign language and having a change of scene, both work and weather, is great. Rather than having one family-sized house, we have two small places – an apartment in London and a small house in southern Spain. Our London flat is in the heart of the inner city, which a lot of people wouldn't like – it's very urban and there's a shortage of open spaces for children. In London we do a lot of cultural stuff – plays, movies, galleries – and Andalucia is a rural contrast. This 'portfolio' lifestyle, where you make a living in a variety of ways rather than sticking to one job, is becoming more popular – though it's not for anyone who wants to get rich. Both of us feel that the fun we've had and the things we've done together in the five years since we've been married have been more fulfilling and rewarding than having a couple of children would have been. While contented parents are prepared to accept that spontaneity will be restricted when their children are young, we felt the restrictions would be too much of a sacrifice.

> If I had children, I would never have been able to do the things I have done in my life, like migrating to Australia, running my own consultancy business, writing books or retiring early as I hope I will do in the future. With children some of these things might have been possible too, but it would certainly have been a lot more difficult or taken a lot more time to accomplish.
>
> *Marije, 28, Sydney*

> We could have lived our married life without children, but I don't think it would have been so much fun!
>
> *Jim, 63, father and grandfather, Glasgow*

Contrary to popular belief, childfree couples tend not to lead fantastically hedonistic lives, flying around in helicopters and spending weekends at luxury hotels. It would be equally misleading to suggest that we're keeping the charitable needs of the world afloat; some do appreciate having the time for community and voluntary activities, but others simply prefer living without children.

Money is often more plentiful in childfree households because both partners can work and aren't implicated in the very high costs of raising children. Some might spend their money on material possessions (as do some parents) but most just appreciate being free of debt and the obligation to grind away at a job they may not like. I've never heard of anyone making a calculated decision not to have children purely on grounds of cost, but raising a family is expensive. Articles are beginning to appear on finance pages in newspapers advising that if you want to have a baby – start saving in your teens.

Following personal dreams, if they're not of the wage-paying kind, is likely to be less possible as a parent. Childfree people often make significant changes in their lives because without dependent children you can afford to take a few months out to consider options. You have the chance to maximise life – there's really no excuse to get stuck in a rut.

Other advantages include being able to travel outside the school holidays, when prices are more reasonable and there are fewer crowds, and living where you like without having to take schools into consideration. Also important is the equality that financial balance, free time and lack of stress bring to a relationship. Happily childfree couples are convinced that their partnerships are enhanced because there are no children.

For many, deciding to remain childfree is a process of self-knowledge that goes to the heart of their identity.

> The best thing about not having children has got to be the quality of life my wife and I enjoy. That translates into having the time and resources to devote to our interests, so we enjoy our time together. I realise for some people the family is their major interest and it's been my observation that these are generally the good parents, who also enjoy their lives.
>
> *P, 42, UK*

Someone once said you need nerves of steel to be a parent, and relief at not being subjected to the worry and anxiety that children can induce also scores highly on the positive list of reasons for not having them. Childfree people tend to be very aware of the realities of parenthood, and are under no illusion that it's easy.

> My husband and I will never lie awake at night waiting for teenagers to come home, wondering if they're in trouble or have been in an accident. There is no guarantee your children will care for you as you care for them. I could not bear the worry and feel sorry for my friends who are going through this.
>
> *Stacey, 45, Philadelphia*

It seems my friends have fallen completely in love, are totally and utterly besotted ... with the most selfish person imaginable who gives very little back but worry and grief. When the child is happy, they are happy, otherwise all is misery. I have never felt anything but relief that I am not in their position.

Joanna, 37, Chester

Many childfree people with jobs don't want to juggle their lives in the hectic manner of their parent colleagues and for some women even the thought of pregnancy, childbirth and breastfeeding is enough to put them off.

Nature is quite something. When I was still breastfeeding William I remember one time when I left him with my husband and went shopping for a couple of hours. I was in Marks and Spencer and I heard a small baby crying. My breasts grew huge – I thought they might burst – and I had to rush home and feed him!

Claire, 39, Kent

I went back to work when I was still breastfeeding. There's something horrible about sitting in a toilet cubicle expressing milk, so I took my breast pump into the boardroom, which is always empty. As I was pumping away the door opened and two male colleagues walked in. I think they were more embarrassed than me.

Sangeeta, 37, London

Some people love doing all the stuff kids like to do, but not everyone relishes the prospect of days spent doing jigsaws or sorting out who pushed who off the swing. Once, my own mum and I watched a mother shove a bag of peanuts in the face of her wailing toddler and shout angrily, 'Eat those and I hope you choke!' Most people can recall bad examples of parenting as well as good. Not everyone's cut out for it.

Although some childfree people don't like children, a significant number like them a lot. Many work with children but have no desire to have their own.

> Freedom, no money worries, peace and quiet, staying young. A tidy home and my body as I like it. I wouldn't have kids for a million pounds! My husband feels the same way.
>
> *Maria, nursery nurse, Cardiff*

A lot of people who choose not to have children feel strongly that human beings are treating the world like seventies rock stars treated their plush hotel rooms. Concerns about the environment and over-population are common, but there's no suggestion (in this book at least) that people shouldn't have children. Creating a family is the raison d'être for a huge number of people – children are a part of our scenery and an integral component of our communities. Babies will always be born. The difficulty is that society pressures people with such relentless determination, both overtly and with stealth, that not to have a baby can make the most robust of adults feel like a social outcast. Until a childfree lifestyle becomes more acceptable, some couples will continue to have children not because they've thought through the tremendous commitment they're undertaking, but simply because it's expected of them. If these people (and they're by no means the majority) were free to follow a path that may suit them better than parenthood, the implications of population growth throughout the world would ease naturally, with benefit to everyone.

It's rare for people in high profile or celebrity positions to speak publicly about their choice to remain childfree because it's controversial, but those that do provide a welcome antidote.

> **I didn't have that desire to be a mother and I don't think a lot of women do. A lot are pressured into it, and they're miserable.**
>
> ***Helen Mirren***

> **What it takes one on one to be a parent, I don't have.**
>
> ***Oprah Winfrey***

Headlines endorsing motherhood as the ultimate achievement are common in the popular press. 'We can predict the most vital date in the life of a woman,' shrieked the tabloids in a story about a scientific formula that predicts the onset of menopause, while on the same day a magazine journalist summarised the life of a successful actress with the phrase: 'While her career is positively glittering, Frances remains both single and childless.' Another sub-editor hedged her bets with the not very catchy, 'High flying careers, exotic holidays and designer clothes are apparently preferred by some women to having kids' – the presence of the word *apparently* suggesting it can't really be true.

Suggesting that the advantages of a childfree life should have a raised profile is not the same as complaining that insufficient coverage is given to a minority sport. Lots of fringe groups moan about being overlooked in the media but it doesn't matter if nobody takes up volleyball. Parenting though is a huge responsibility that impacts on the whole of society.

> I wish someone would explain it to me – what is the big deal about being a parent? I don't hate children, I like their curiosity and honesty, but I just turned 35 and feel absolutely no desire to have my own. Sometimes I think something is wrong with me. I find myself feeling sorry for mothers.
>
> *Daisy, USA*

The u-turn in social attitudes in the last half century, coupled with more recent hype that's made anything to do with babies and children A Wonderful Thing, has made pregnancy acceptable almost whatever your circumstances. But it's put young women on the receiving end of conflicting messages. Teenage motherhood is not condoned, but magazine racks are stacked with pictures of famous mums and beautiful babies while there's little mention of positive alternatives to parenthood.

> I am 17 and I live in a small town in Virginia. We get lots of sex education in school and through the

church, but lots of girls I know have babies already. The women involved in the sex education are horrified when girls of my age get pregnant. They throw up their hands and cry 'Babies are having babies!' as though it's a terrible thing. Then, by the flash of a bureaucratic wand, you become an adult on your 18th birthday. You leave school and the message changes completely. There is no sex education any more and babies are suddenly seen as a blessing – the greatest gift on earth. The sex-ed teachers drop you like a sack of old potatoes. Not to want a baby would be unthinkable. It is very confusing.

Krystal, 17, USA

Motherhood is still thought of as the female nirvana, even though women spent the last century campaigning for the right to be freed from the shackles of their gender. History tells us of the grind that was womanhood and though modern conveniences have reset the stage on which child rearing is performed, any candid 21st-century mum will tell you about the daily exhaustion of raising her young.

You have to really want children. If you don't, then don't have them. They're wonderful, but it's bloody hard work and your life will not be the same as it was before.

Siri, Granada, Spain

My grandmother had six children and is now in her eighties. She tells me how she used to wait until

> Grandpa was asleep before she'd go to bed. In her day getting pregnant wasn't a choice. Thank God it is now.
>
> *Lesley, 35, Winchester*

Thousands of years of tradition have left their mark upon women. It seems there's an almost subconscious desire to prove a maternal instinct and even those who are happily childless are not exempt. 'I may not have a child, but look, I know what to do!' we proclaim, if subconsciously, in the company of friends with small children. Hands are outstretched with eager readiness if a child strays within football-pitch distance of a staircase, and there's a universally recognised code of tender hair stroking should he bump into your legs. Having the child take a shine to you is rather like catching the bridal bouquet. You're vindicated! He likes you! You've proved your womanly worth. While these emotional undercurrents circulate around the child, his real mother – who has of course proved her maternal ability – is most likely to be found having a fag in the back garden, grateful there are so many watchful eyes for once. When men interact with children they don't appear to be seeking approval in the same way.

If women do behave with indifference towards children, it brings to the fore the fact that roles are being questioned on a fundamental level, which may help to explain the unease that surrounds the childfree debate. If women don't want to have babies, the big life questions of Why We Are Here and What We Are For become more unfathomable.

> There's a very pervasive attitude that you haven't really fulfilled your potential (especially if you're

> female) and that you haven't developed fully unless you've had a baby. Women in previous generations fought long and hard for our rights, and one of those rights was to be able to have a choice – that being female wasn't just about being a mother. It seems like we've thrown it all away. Yes you can work, have a career and be financially independent, but you still have to have children to be 'complete'.
>
> *Alex, 41, civil servant*

It's not always easy to be in a minority, especially one that everyone seems determined to challenge, but it is liberating to feel that you made up your own mind. If in years to come being childfree has an upbeat, un-extraordinary image, maybe it will make life easier for those who don't have children but didn't choose it that way too.

Jim and I came to our decision as we sat watching the sun go down on the stone ruins of Chichen Itza in Mexico. The 2,000-year-old stepped pyramid was built by the Mayans with such accuracy and placed with such minute consideration of its relation to the sun that, one day a year on the summer solstice, the evening shadows cast patterns down its sides that appear as huge snakes. Ultimately our decision to remain childfree was easy; we couldn't imagine missing out on all the world's wonders.

Marcelle d'Argy Smith
writer; former editor, *Cosmopolitan*
b 1947

I've always aimed to do things that enrich my life and, because I've managed to do those things, I've liked my life enough never to want to alter it by having children. I always wanted to get out there and see the world and I could never have done that if I'd been tied. I used to jump on a plane at a moment's notice and go to work in New York. You can leave the dishes but you can't leave the kids! Now that I'm older I can go to that party in the Hamptons, I can shut myself in a room and write for three days, I can crawl into bed and see nobody for a long weekend or I can sod off to South Africa – I might think I don't want to spend the money on all the airfares, but I can go if I want.

If I'd been a man or a millionaire it would have been wonderful to have lots of children scurrying around, but I'm practical and realistic. I'd need a house like Brideshead and hoards of staff to look after us all, but most of us don't have lives like that and I certainly never wanted a man to provide it for me. Fathers are often happy because they have wonderful jobs, their own lives and children as well, but it's not like that for mothers.

I wouldn't have compromised a relationship for the sake of having children so I got on with doing my own life and the advantages are tremendous. I always wanted to look at a partner and think I truly, truly love you. I am shocked by the number of women who marry for status, convenience or to be accepted socially.

I never had the urge to reproduce me – there are too many abandoned children in the world. So many children need love and attention – they don't have to be your own. My maternal instincts come out in different ways. I teach creative writing to young adults and you can fall in love with your class. They write their little hearts out, they confide in you, they tell you things they don't tell their parents. I adore them.

I have been called selfish and it makes me incandescent with rage. Blood is not thicker than water. Single people have a fantastically strong support network and we help each other. You dare not call parents at the weekend – that's family time!

Most of my friends with kids have become more honest as we've got older. They say I've had a far more varied and interesting time than they have. People like to perpetuate rituals of birth, marriage and death – it is how people conform but it would never have suited me. My own mother used to ask when I'd get married and have babies until I began editing *Cosmo*. Then she marched up and down the high street with copies of the magazine under her arm telling people 'this is my daughter, you know'. She never asked about marriage and children again.

When I was small she was stuck at home. You don't realise when you are a child how hellish it is for the person bringing you up. My father used to say to me 'why on earth would you want to get married?' He described himself as a bachelor with a wife and children. He'd get halfway through Christmas and disappear. Mothers do not have that option. As a mother you pour your whole self into your kids. You train them, you teach them, you love them and supposedly you let them go, although parents are bad at that – more like octopuses really with tentacles that reach out and complain; 'you didn't visit' or 'you forgot my birthday'. I hate all that.

One of my closest friends has been married three times and has three children. She says, 'It's amazing Marce, you have to get married to realise it isn't necessary and you have to have children to realise you

don't need them'. She adores her girls but her life is not her own. I love my life so much I count myself lucky every single day.

You won't regret not having children, you absolutely won't. You can do whatever you want to do. You can't put a price on freedom. People die for the right to be free.

Chapter 2
The Childfree Stigma

I tell people I can't have children because
it stops them always asking
Why? Why? Why? I don't want to have them.
Cornelia, Switzerland

If you mention you don't want kids in the company of parents an unsolicited opinion is guaranteed. Only very occasionally will people acknowledge the remark without fuss before the conversation moves on to something more interesting. Reactions can be positive and encouraging, but more common is a mix of hostility and defensiveness followed by lots of probing questions. Pity on behalf of the parent towards the non-parent is not uncommon, even when the non-parent clarifies that their choice is entirely voluntary. There is really no need to feel sorry for us!

There is nothing sadder than a childless couple. It breaks my heart to see them relaxing around swimming pools in Florida, sitting all suntanned and miserable on the decks of their boats, trotting off to Europe like lonesome fools. It's an empty life. Nothing but money to spend, more time to enjoy and a whole lot less to worry about.

The poor childless couple are so wrapped up in themselves you have to feel sorry for them. They don't fight over the child's discipline, don't blame each other for the child's most obnoxious characteristics and they miss all the fun of doing without for the child's sake. They just go along, doing whatever they want, buying what they want and liking each other. It's a pretty pathetic picture.

Everyone should have children. No one should be allowed to escape the wonderful experience that accompanies each stage in the development of the young. The happy memories of sleepless nights, coughing spells, tantrums, diaper rash, saturated mattresses, emergencies, debts and never-ending crises.

How dismal is the peaceful home without the constant childish problems that make for a well-rounded life and an early breakdown. The tender, thoughtful discussions when the report card reveals the progeny to be one step below a moron. The end-of-the-day reunions with all the joyful happenings recited like well-placed blows to the temples.

> **The childless couple live in a vacuum. They fill their lonely days with golf, vacations, dinner dates, civic affairs, tranquility, leisure and entertainment. There is a terrifying emptiness without children, but the childless couple are too comfortable to know it.**
>
> **You just have to look at them to see what the years have done: He looks boyish, unlined and rested. She's slim, well-groomed and youthful. It isn't natural. If they had kids, they'd look like the rest of us. Worn out, wrinkled and exhausted.**
>
> **The Childless Couple *by an unknown US author***

Childfree people do not have the need to endlessly question parents – the fact that people have children is not an issue to us. It shouldn't matter how one finds purpose in life – if it's kids fine, if it's origami fine. But tension is inevitable when those who comply with the social norm attempt to portray anyone different as a misfit.

Betty Friedan, who wrote *The Feminine Mystique* in the 1960s, said that when you separate a woman from her fertility you have to accept her for what she is, rather than for her ability to reproduce. She reckoned that was the reason anger is sometimes directed at contentedly childless women.

Dealing with judgemental people is one of the very few disadvantages of being childfree. Several contributors to this book wanted their identities kept secret because they feared the fallout of candidly talking about their lives.

> I can't afford to have my name or my company name mentioned. It's been my experience that some people are threatened by our lifestyle and can be hostile.
>
> *O, 42, UK*

People want everything to be black or white – either you desperately want a baby or you vehemently don't – but real lives are more the shade of whites-mixed-with-colours on a too hot cycle. Childfree people aren't sitting in darkened rooms sticking pins in fabric dolls or prowling the streets like the child-catcher in *Chitty Chitty Bang Bang*. Some have always been certain they never wanted kids, but others considered both options before plumping not to. My own analogy is that I chose the chocolate cake over the flapjack. It doesn't mean I wouldn't have liked the flapjack, but I like the chocolate cake better.

In self-effacing company both parents and non-parents can discuss the consequences of their big life choices without any acrimony, but it only happens with those who have confidence that they've made the right decision for themselves. Realistic parents share their kids' less than joyous moments and laugh in turn at my odd tales of humiliation brought about by being childfree. ('Here is the sad, sad lady who has no babies!' an Egyptian waiter serenaded loudly across a restaurant when I appeared for dinner alone one night.)

Some parents are truly evangelical about their children and simply want to spread the word about how wonderful parenthood is, but to the childfree person it feels like they have an agenda. Heterosexual people don't harp on to gay people about how great their sex lives are after all. Other parents have genuine religious beliefs ('go forth and multiply') and there are those who are just plain envious of the freedoms enjoyed by people without children. Maybe they didn't consider that they had an option too.

> These people without children don't realise how hard being a mother is. It is our duty to be there for our children and that means exceptions must be made sometimes. Time off work is a good example. When these non-parents become parents, they will have a better understanding of how much a mother has to do.
>
> *Deborah, 39*

Note the use of the word 'when', rather than 'if' in the final sentence.

> You get extraordinary reactions when you are childfree. I remember going round to a friend's house about 11 o'clock one Sunday morning. She was in the back garden so I spoke to her husband first. He asked what I'd been doing that morning and I told him I hadn't been awake for that long. He looked appalled and said he'd been up since 7 o'clock and taken three children swimming already. He wasn't laughing and saying 'it's all right for some!' He implied he'd been fulfilling a moral duty and I hadn't.
>
> *Lesley, 35, Winchester*

> One of our relatives who has four children came to stay. We took her and her husband out to dinner

> and listened enthusiastically while they told us all about the kids' latest exploits. When we got back to our house, which my partner and I had spent the last 18 months rebuilding, she looked around the newly finished kitchen and said, 'People who don't have children have nothing better to do than eat out and shop.' I swallowed my rage and replied, 'Yes, I know, it's wonderful!'
>
> *Jan, 40, London*

Heated conversations about being childfree unfortunately tend to take place at social gatherings where people don't know each other and are wading their way through typical introductory questions. I don't mind being asked if I have children – it's a question I ask others myself – but I do mind being criticised for my decision when I'd rather be relaxing. If someone tells me they have children, I always take a genuine interest and sometimes feel that I'm bending over backwards to ensure the conversation is congenial, but most parents think nothing of offering their own, often highly charged views. I've been the reluctant subject of countless one-way invectives, though in a social or personal setting I wouldn't dream of questioning an individual parent's decision to have had children. How rude would it seem if I were to say, 'You have kids? You're so misguided!' Yet it happens, routinely, in reverse. Even if the dialogue is calm, a childfree person can spend hours, cocktail sausage in hand, enquiring politely about schools and swimming lessons while the parent concerned asks not one question about the childfree person's life. A typical conversation might follow a pattern of the parent (nearly always female) praising her own offspring to unlikely heights before telling the childfree person that she's 'missing out'. Often the mother will say you're 'protesting too much' if you insist you don't want kids, but mention you might sometimes wonder about the pleasures of family life and you'll be told the *admission* reveals that you're in denial. The childfree person is stuck, like Jordan, between Iraq and a hard place.

Even when you've done your utmost to make it clear, some women cannot accept that you don't want a child. Such determined persuaders are like matronly mothers-in-law who won't take no for an answer when you decline a helping of pudding. 'Go on, just one little slice, you must want a tiny taste?' they croon (not that a 'tiny taste' of baby is an option). If you still refuse they are wounded or huffy, as though a personal slight has been made against their children, or their treacle sponge.

Sometimes, when a mother has spent a long time telling me how I'll 'miss out', I ask why it matters if I don't want a baby. Perhaps I should feel touched at her concern for my welfare, except that the reply to this question is always a haughty, 'Well it doesn't matter, *to me*.' It doesn't matter to me that she has a baby either, but then I don't feel compelled to keep asking why she's got one.

Sometimes if a childfree person admires a toddler or praises the achievements of a teenager, parents see it as a chance to exploit what they see as a weakness. 'It could have been you,' they say with an indulgent sigh, 'but of course, you chose something ... alternative.' What a sad world it is if paying a simple compliment provokes a loaded reaction, and how ridiculous to suggest that if a childfree person is kind about someone's children it means they're questioning their decision not to have had their own.

Childfree people aren't overly bothered about the 'bonuses' that children bring or they wouldn't be childfree, and that's perhaps where the tension lies because parents *do* miss some of the things they enjoyed before the kids came along. If they only miss them to a minor degree they won't be upset by stories of free time and less responsibility. But defensiveness kicks in when envy plays a part. It's bad enough to feel envious of something over which you had no control, but if looking back you see that you could have lived a different life, the envy could intensify.

> I never had my own children because I didn't want them, but I am getting married next year to a man who has three boys aged from eight to seventeen. Some women I know can't conceal their delight that now, finally, I'm going to 'find out what it's like'.
>
> *Joella, 44, step-mum-in-waiting, Australia*

As part of my research I spent the day with volunteers and staff at the parents' support charity Parentline Plus. They speak in more detail in Chapter 11, but I was particularly curious to find out if they had any thoughts why parents so often take against childfree people.

I don't have a particular theory. Having children is not a rational decision so it may be unusual for parents to meet someone who doesn't share that

primal urge. There may be some envy because parents give up a lot for their children. Most choices that we make in our lives are reversible. A job can be left, a house can be sold, but you cannot give a child back. There is no right or wrong with having children or not having children, but you make a choice and you go with it. There will be good points and bad points about both options. Parentline Plus believes parenthood is a choice.

Gill Loughran, deputy chief executive, Parentline Plus

The dynamic of being married but childfree confuses people immensely. At a barbecue once I was told that I *invited* criticism if I openly mentioned I was childfree by choice. 'You can't expect people to carry on chatting and ignore what you've said!' a friend of a friend admonished as though I'd announced I ate babies for breakfast. I pointed out that not long ago polite conversation over the sausages would have faltered if someone had said they were gay. Hopefully it won't be too long before childfree people are met with affable indifference, but given that this was a relaxed occasion in a cosmopolitan suburb of London I won't be holding my breath.

Prospective grandparents can be very cutting too, and as much to singles as couples:

While visiting my mum in Australia we went to a party next door. I was the youngest person there and one woman was complaining that she really wanted grandchildren, but she didn't know when

> her daughter – who was only in her early twenties – was going to have them. She then turned to me and said pointedly, 'It's women like you, who choose their career over children, who are responsible.' Then she asked my mother, 'Don't you want grandchildren too?' I was so upset to be attacked in this way, particularly as I *do* want children but haven't yet met the right man to father them.
>
> *Josephine, 34, PR*

Other people visibly flounder when they meet a woman who says she doesn't want a child and over-compensate embarrassingly in an effort to demonstrate *just how okay* they are with that. 'Oh, I know what you mean,' one mother chummed up, 'When mine were small I wanted to smash their heads against the wall and put pillows over their faces.' Later in the conversation guilt inevitably caught up with her and she launched into a long diatribe about how much she loves her children.

Yet more party guests try to cover being flummoxed with hapless compliments that could be likened to a woman wearing a sari being told, 'You're exotic.'

Mothers are the fiercest critics of childfree women. A single woman who chooses to have a baby by ingenious methods is accepted, certainly in London, with greater ease than a married one who doesn't want kids. Even seemingly progressive mums are intrigued by my own childfree position and the subject is bound to come up during the course of an evening out. Food and wine are accompanied by chatter that ranges from work to war, but at some point even the closest of female friends will pop in a question that checks if I've changed my mind and decided to get pregnant yet. Ladies, get out of those twin sets.

For all but the supremely self-assured, not having kids can result in a bit of harmless self-analysis. If everyone keeps telling you how fantastic something is, it would be arrogant not to wonder if they might have a point, and I've sat on a late bus home a few times wondering if I could be missing out on something. But ruffled feelings settle back into their state of contented conviction pretty quickly. By the next morning when I wake up in my own time and contemplate what to do with my day, I always feel glad that I was the odd one out around the dinner table.

Convention has narrow boundaries and it's not only child-free status that gives rise to moral indignation. Two point four children is no longer the mean birth rate in the western world but most people seem to think it is and parents of single children also get questioned about their reasons for having just one, sometimes with a suggestion that they're selfish not to provide a sibling-playmate. Hillary and Bill Clinton faced endless speculation about the validity of their marriage and commitment to family long before the Lewinsky affair, and the UK's Chancellor of the Exchequer Gordon Brown was treated as a curious aberration in public politics before he married and had his children. Tanni Grey-Thompson says she got a more bizarre response to being pregnant in a wheelchair than she did to being an Olympic athlete in a wheelchair, and a divorced friend of mine, whose two children live abroad with their Dad (her ex-husband) and his new wife, faces inferences that the courts must have 'taken them away'. In fact the living arrangements simply suit everyone best. Family life is still portrayed as Mum, Dad and a couple of Colgate kids – one boy, one girl, all tucked under the same roof.

In 1967 the world's first heart transplant caused outrage among people who considered it immoral. Forty years on, such surgery is far from unique, but equal discomfort is now being directed toward breakthroughs in women's fertility. When Paul McCartney, Michael Douglas and Des O'Connor became fathers in their sixties and seventies they were congratulated – smiling photographs of them appeared in our newspapers. But the few women who've become pregnant in their fifties and sixties as a result of fertility treatment are regarded almost like monsters. The childfree idea too is new.

Today's young women are the first to be taking an analytical approach to motherhood, but it's not surprising some are beginning to do so. Not only are alternative opportunities greater than they were for our mothers, but those opportunities have brought with them modern complexities that were unheard of in previous generations.

On holiday in tropical countries I'm not in the least fazed when I'm asked how many children I have because there are only two possible answers in the questioner's mind. Either I haven't had children yet or I'm unable to have them at all. On a beach in Goa, Mira, who made her living giving massages to pasty skinned tourists, responded to my saying I had no children by slopping vats of coconut oil on my tummy and rubbing vigorously to help things along. It was great – but I wouldn't expect it at home.

Zoe Williams
journalist
b 1973

I wrote an article about the culture of parenthood and the response was huge.

Lots of readers contacted the magazine but the comments were all about whether people should have children or not, which wasn't the point. People seem programmed to reduce intellectual arguments to a base level and the interesting elements get hijacked, simplified and polarised. One reader whose letter appeared the following week wrote that anyone who doesn't have children should agree to voluntary euthanasia as soon as they become non-productive members of society. He said I was relying on his children to support me in my old age!

ND: Why are opinions so divided?

I think women are unsupportive of each other and maybe that's why achieving equality takes so long. Historically, for every woman who's stood up for her rights and made clear that she cannot be boiled down to her ability to reproduce, there have been ten more standing on the touchline telling her she's letting the side down.

Everyone seems very prescriptive these days, which I think is a modern trend. No one thinks twice about giving you their unsolicited views, especially regarding children, and everyone wants an endorsement that you are doing things the same way as they are. Parents want their childfree friends to become parents too. That develops into divided opinion on whether the mother should work or not and then comes the private school versus state school debate.

ND: But there's no right and wrong on whether one should have children?

That's true. You can do the right thing and it not be the same as everyone else. It's incredibly patronising for people to suggest otherwise. I haven't decided about children yet, but there are no other major decisions in my life that I have made and then regretted. I knew when I was a child that I loved dogs and I still do. I knew in my early teens that I was a socialist and I still am.

ND: Do people have children for sound reasons?

It's like Pascal's wager with God* isn't it? Even if you're not sure He exists you might as well believe anyway because it doesn't do you any harm. If it turns out He does exist you get to go to heaven. People don't know if they'll regret not having children so they have them anyway, because they know they'll love them and so the possibility of regret is erased.

ND: Are women with children very different to women without children?

Not that I can tell. They might drink a bit less I suppose. Mothers are quick to claim that children change their lives in a miraculous way and there are those that imply that childfree women lead selfish and indulgent lives. But I haven't noticed that beauty salons, hairdressers and Harvey Nichols are empty of mothers.

ND: Why do people want everyone to be the same as they are?

It's the product of an increasingly conservative society. People are suspicious of anyone who's not the same as them – whether it's a person from a different religious background or a child on an adoption list. There's an IVF frenzy because people must have 'their own' baby.

*

	God exists	God does not exist
Wager for God	Gain all	Status quo
Wager against God	Misery	Status quo

Blaise Pascal b 1623, Clermont, France. Physicist, mathematician and writer on religious issues

It would be very rare for parents to consider taking on someone else's child in place of recreating their own flesh and blood. Although it's changing on the surface, the relationship of friends is undervalued too, hence comments to childfree people about 'when you're old it's family you'll need'. Friendships are valued less than family because people are still more trusting of 'what's theirs'.

ND: Why?

I think it's a result of our moral universe getting smaller and people becoming more disengaged in politics. Financially you can do anything these days and it's not questioned. You can buy a second home in a rural village which prices local people out of the market and employ a cleaner which creates a social underclass. The politics of such decisions might be discussed in newspapers occasionally, but the people making them are either oblivious to the politics or don't care. When they have children, a parent's political morality flies out the window because everything they do can be followed up by 'it's because we want the best for Billy'. Suppose that pre-parenthood you supported the idea of state education, but once your child reaches five you send him to a private school? You can just say 'we weren't going to make our child a political pawn'. There is no collective social responsibility anymore.

And I don't want to sound bonkers but the environment is another issue ...

ND: You're not bonkers, I've just written a whole chapter about it.

Right well, all our grandchildren will be doing is picking up our rubbish, it'll be hell.

Chapter 3
Parent Propaganda

Selfishness is not living as one wishes to live,
it is asking others to live as one wishes to live.
Oscar Wilde

Well-meaning parents empathise with childfree people by saying that they never wanted children until they had their own, which only makes me think *que*? Plenty want to share their Damascene conversion stories, while others are members of the mummy mafia who subject childfree people to powerful Parent Propaganda. The top ten:

1. It's selfish not to have children

Wrong. Parents have children because they want them, not for the greater good of society. Resulting self-sacrifice is nothing more than enlightened self-interest. Mothers get involved in child-orientated events because they benefit their own children; fathers referee mini-soccer matches because their kids are in the league. Parents who spend hours in the car driving their children from Brownies to music lessons to sleepovers chose that life for themselves. Hopefully their children appreciate it, but it's an inward looking generosity not worthy of widespread martyrdom.

Some parents can be selfish. A colleague in her late thirties faces endless questions from her parents about why she 'can't find a husband' – hardly a generous sentiment. She was distraught when her father wrote on a Christmas present list 'grandchildren and a pair of gardening gloves'.

The record for my own selfishness being inferred by a complete stranger is less than 20 seconds. After introducing herself and pointing to her children (sadly indistinguishable to me among the others on the bouncy castle), my new acquaintance asked how many *squinks* I'd brought along to the party we were at. 'None,' I said, 'we decided not to have children.' She did a fair impression of a beached fish before spluttering, 'Isn't that rather self-centred?'

Childfree people prioritise differently, often by turning their attention to other deserving matters, of which there are plenty apart from one's own children. Having more time allows us to take primary care of older family members and a lack of personal restrictions means we're often called upon first in a crisis. Many do choose to work in the community which, like parenthood, is both useful for others *and* fulfilling to ourselves. Few people are truly altruistic, and they can be parents or non-parents.

2. You'll change your mind

This is even offered in advice to childfree women who are rapidly approaching the menopause. I've been told I'll be queuing up at the Cambodian Embassy waving adoption papers when I'm 45, and if I am – great. But demographic research shows that childfree adults are likely to be educated and affluent with careers and nice lives.[1] We've made good decisions in other important areas so there's no reason this should be different.

> I worried at the time that everyone might be right – it was very unusual not to have a child when I was young. The regret never happened, I've had a wonderful life.
>
> *Kathleen, Queensland, Australia*
> *(who asked me not to reveal her exact age,*
> *only that she's in her eighties!)*

To embark on parenthood if you're unconvinced, simply to safeguard against possible future regret, seems absurd. I could have grown-up children myself already. I'm not sorry that I don't.

3. People who don't have children aren't normal

By a stroke of coincidence I was told that it's abnormal for women not to want babies at a reception held in the Natural History Museum, overlooked by the huge Diplodocus in the foyer. The man with whom I was sharing my canapés stared at me warily, as though my insides might be filled with wires and circuit boards. When I asked him if all tall men should be basketball players he paused rather touchingly before concluding, 'No, but men can do other things.'

It's often implied, though never with compassion, that childfree people opt out of parenthood because they are psychologically (if not physically) flawed, or have troubled pasts. It may be the case sometimes, but it doesn't take a degree in the law of averages to work out that just as many parents have less than rosy histories too.

(3.a) Childfree people also get told that **Only parents are true adults** – a concept quickly dismissed by a friend who recalls that the first time she went out after the birth of her daughter, she got so drunk she came home and was sick on the living room carpet.

4. There'll be nobody to look after you when you're old

The numbers of people in western society who care full-time for their elderly parents is relatively small.[2] Many are ambivalent about the role.

> **The French Government is to punish families who fail to keep in touch with elderly relatives after being shamed by statistics that reveal that the suicide rate among its pensioners is the highest in Europe. In a country that prides itself on traditional Catholic family values, elderly people left to fend for themselves are committing suicide at a rate of 62 a week, according to figures released last week. The move comes just six months after 15,000**

> **mostly elderly people died in last summer's heat-wave, only for their bodies to lie unclaimed for weeks while their families enjoyed their annual holidays.**
>
> *World Press Reports, February 2004*

In Italy, which we tend to consider a family-orientated nation, nearly 50 per cent of pensioners live alone. Eighty-year-old Giorgio Angelozzi put himself up for adoption in 2004 because he was so lonely. His only daughter had moved abroad and he's now happily settled with a new family in Milan, where he moved from Rome.

Many childfree people consider having children as an insurance policy against one's own old age – a poor and selfish reason in itself.

5. It's different when they're your own

If all your life you've had no interest in animals, would you apply for a job in a cat sanctuary? Parents often admit that they're not interested in other people's children, only their own, which not only smacks of protectionism but says little for their broader social responsibility (see 3.a).

Parents might walk through flames or drown in icy waters for the sake of their kids but a lot of childfree people, though perfectly capable of loving relationships, feel comfortable with more rational emotions.

> If I had a dollar for everyone who told me 'it's different when they're your own,' I'd be a wealthy woman. I spend a lot of time with my three

> nephews. It's true, I don't mind standing in queues at Disneyworld with them or taking a half hour to decide what cookies they want to buy in the store because it's worth it to see the pleasure on their faces. But the boys are not 'my own' and I don't believe my feelings have anything to do with the fact that their mom is my sister. It's just that I know them well, as anyone can get to know a child.
>
> *Lottie, 50, insurance clerk, Tampa, Florida*

6. Childfree people are uptight, anally retentive perfectionists who 'couldn't cope' with kids (Ogod. Should anally retentive have a hyphen?)

Children are great levellers, for sure. When I boasted at a family gathering that I'd written a thousand words before anyone else got up in the morning, my nephew who's six remarked dismissively that some of them were the same words, so it didn't really count. His mum, my sister-in-law, has childfree friends who can spend half an hour fretting in the Sainsbury's fresh produce aisle if there's no organic rocket on the shelves. Should they take the non-organic, or park their trolley neatly and drive across town to see if Tesco's has any? Oddly, parents seem to think that couples like this should acquire some children to force them to get a perspective on life, but the presence of small, sticky fingers in a just-so household would merely make everyone miserable, so what's the point?

Do Jim and I glide around our apartment in an atmosphere of saintly calm, stroking our pristine work surfaces and admiring our co-ordinated sock drawer? We don't, more's the pity – and for the record, chairing an important meeting and subsequently discovering that you did so with fromage frais dribbled on your cardie is not the exclusive predilection of the busy working mum.

7. You chose a career instead of children

This is particularly annoying for anyone who would have liked to have children but was perhaps unlucky in love. 'What was I meant to do?' a friend asks, 'sit in a chair doing needlepoint until Mr Right showed up?' Childfree people often do well in interesting jobs, but reducing work commitments has become popular in recent years as people in all social circumstances seek out a better quality of life.

> I have a good job, but I opted to work part-time recently because I wanted to improve my life-work balance. I won't be in line for promotion, but I'm happier now because I'm exploring new avenues. I can manage financially because there is only me to look after. For years I wanted to learn to sail and that's my plan for next summer.
>
> *Abby, 40, finance manager, Manchester*

8. Childfree women are cold and un-nurturing

'Don't you like kids?' is a lazy assumption. Many children are blessed with endearing qualities, but if you think they all are you should probably examine your own skills of judgement. Women who choose not to have children don't hate them but, unlike many of their parents, are prepared to accept they won't all grow up to be doctors and charity workers. Given a free day most childfree people would opt for a gallery over Legoland, but plenty enjoy children's company – if for short periods of time.

A significantly high number of people who took part in research for this book work as teachers and carers. A childless Head Teacher of the Year described her job as 'her baby'. Over a number of years, she devotedly transformed a failing inner-city Primary into a happy and productive place of learning.

Florence Nightingale had no children and, in this quote, refers to her experiences nursing the soldiers of the Crimean War:

> **The real fathers and mothers of the human race are not the fathers and mothers of the flesh. For every one of my 18,000 children, I have expended more motherly feeling and action in a week than my mother has expended on me in 37 years.**
>
> ***Florence Nightingale, 1820–1910*[3]**

There's no shortage of outlets for nurturing tendencies, even for those who don't like children per se. A lot of child-free people have a strong affinity with animals. Not all mothers are nurturing and not all non-mothers are un-nurturing.

9. Your life needn't change when you have children!

First-time mums and dads attempt to recruit Jim and me to parenthood with the determination of pyramid sellers on a high rate of commission. They're keen to insist that our trips abroad could segue seamlessly from banana boats up the Amazon to a fortnight in Centerparcs without us even noticing. 'You *can* travel with children,' they plead, and always come up with a tale of a family of five who sold their house and sailed round the world in a reclaimed dinghy when the children were small. I can't think of anything worse. Often we hear that we *just don't get* what having kids is about, but it could be the other way round. Jim especially is the sort of person who would hypothetically strap a baby on his back and cart it around the jungle, no fuss. But, soaked-in and sharing the sights and sounds of a new foreign culture, it's the being *just us* that appeals when we're travelling. The real motivation behind these comments is that of a bridegroom who, fearing a loss of fun and freedom, baits his footloose Best Man that *he should be next*.

10. Your life without children will be empty and unfulfilled

'Life gets a bit thin without children, after age 40,' Martin Amis remarked at a party. And some of your novels get thin after *page* 40, I thought indignantly. If you decide not to have children in your late thirties there's room for all those things you haven't had time for in the 20-odd years you've been busy at work. Parents who say that their lives would be worthless without their kids discard the value of their own existence before the children were born. In the interview he did with Melvyn Bragg shortly before he died, the playwright Dennis Potter talked of *seeing the blossom* for the very first time. Meaning can be found wherever you look for it and to savour that privilege ahead of the grim reaper casting his shadow is fulfilment aplenty for some of us.

Families have snapshots of their children to look through, but childless singles and couples sew their own Bayeux tapestry of memories. Parents are mesmerised by their children's development, but the profundity of nature is all around for the curious few to observe and absorb. In Beijing Zoo, Jim and I lounged on the grass close up to the Giant Pandas for so long that their behaviour convinced us that they were a hoax – furry suits with zips up the back and out-of-work actors inside. All those parents who cast them just a fleeting glance on their way to the ice-cream tent missed out. The world is the childfree person's adventure playground.

> Those people who suggest you'll have this great emptiness if you don't have children are writing off 99 per cent of the gay population. We get different propaganda to childfree women – nobody wants us to have children (well it's not right, is it?). My life is fun, full and happy and it's the same for most of my gay friends, though Pete's a bit of a misery, now I come to think of it. People slip into having children as an outlet for pent up creativity. They create a child, whereas I've created lots of other interesting projects. I ran a design business for several years which did well, but I sold it when I was 40 because I felt like a change. I invested the proceeds in a run down house and refurbished it to its original Georgian glory. Now I'm into art. I've had the freedom and money to do all these things and make friends from all walks of life. Six years ago I trained

as airline cabin crew and I now work part-time on long haul flights. The money is a perk but it's more a life-enhancing project. I get to fly all over the world, relax in beautiful hotels, shop or see the sights in countries I might never have visited. Most colleagues I fly with have families to support. Once I was stuffing dirty meal trays into a trolley at four o'clock in the morning when a passenger remarked, 'Now I bet you wish you'd worked harder at school'. I can laugh or I can leave, but any job's a burden if you have to stick it for the money. As for company, I've loads of friends. People who think children are the only true reward in life must have had a rather a dull time.

Jonty, 53, entrepreneur

Ask any propagandist if they'd make these remarks to an infertile couple and they'll shake their heads vigorously (because *that* would be insensitive). There are so many unexamined beliefs about parenthood. I know we're supposed to rise above it, but rise any higher and we'll look like giraffes.

'Private Lives'

Guardian, 11 January 2002

(Each week, 'Private Lives' features a reader's personal dilemma. Other readers write in with advice and suggestions.)

We are trying to decide if we should remain child-free. We are both professionals in our late 30s and married in the spring. If we are to have children, then time is pressing. We have read all the 'having the child in later life' books, and remaining child-free seems an attractive option! While enjoying the company of other people's children, neither of us feels a strong urge to become a parent. However, there is doubt at the back of our minds that by not even trying we might be missing something, and regret it in later life. All the parents we have asked tell us that the worry, toil, heartache, expense and pain are 'worth it in the end'. The lack of any dissenting voice makes us deeply suspicious! Are there any couples who have had children and then regretted the decision, or is parenthood the only way to true fulfilment?

Name and address withheld

Trust your instincts

When in doubt, don't. Don't allow yourselves to be pressured into something you don't really want to do, and especially don't fall for the 'selfish' line – those who choose to have children do so for entirely selfish reasons, not altruistic ones, and you are not being selfish if you choose differently.

It's true that there are rewards (but then your friends have to convince themselves of the wisdom of their decision – and are anxious that you don't escape to a different life). I became a parent reluctantly, and

always knew I'd made the wrong decision. My child is now a fine and loving adult, and does not know that secretly I still terribly regret letting myself think I ought to go along with the prevailing customs. I would have been a far happier person as a non-parent.

The world is over-populated anyway – why procreate just because you think you ought?

Name and address withheld

Benefit of hindsight

Like you, we were uncertain about having children. I had spent all of my younger years convinced I didn't want them. However, in our mid-30s we had our first of two children, now a teenager.

If I had known how having children would make me feel, I wouldn't have had them, so presumably my earlier reservations were somewhat justified.

Children have to fit into an existing relationship, so they are bound to create a wedge to some extent.

The biological 'rub' is that you can never truly know in advance how you will respond to this mammoth event. If we did, not many of us would reproduce.

Having said all this, it would destroy me completely if anything happened to my children.

Name and address withheld

Don't believe the hype

I am a parent, although I had always known that I didn't want to have children. When confronted aged 40 by a dearly beloved wife who decided she did want children, I had to choose between leaving her and capitulating.

Now, with the children in their teens, and all going quite well, most people assume I've changed my mind, but I haven't. Not because I don't love them – I do, as much as any parent – but because I preferred

the freedom of our lives before we had them, and because I still feel bad about having contributed to the world's overpopulation.

'It's worth it in the end,' say your friends. Yes, when they're grown-up, certainly, and from about 5 to 10 years old when they're quite magical, the brief interregnum between nappies and attitude, but the rest of it can be quite a slog. Your present life of spontaneous decisions, freedom to make plans together regardless of suppertime or school holidays, freedom not to take unrewarding work because you can afford a few months without salary – all replaced by the tyranny of the school timetable, homework, and the children's need for domestic regularity.

Fine for those who actively want that, but if you're doubtful, don't believe the propaganda. It's the same story as married men persuading bachelors to take the plunge – they don't mean it, they just can't bear anybody to escape the chains as they didn't.

Name and address withheld

I haven't missed out

I spent several years wondering whether to have children, even though I have experienced only rare maternal desires. In the end it occurred to me that child bearing is instinctive and I was missing the point. If I had wanted to have children I would have had them. I am now 40, have fibroids, am missing an ovary, the doctors suspect that I am going into early menopause, and the thing that I feared, that I would want children when it was too late, has not happened.

Gill Whelan, Aberdeen

The richest experience

There are times when all parents regret having children; the sleepless nights, tantrum toddlers, teenagers from hell. But ultimately there are few who would ever

say it has not 'been worth it'. Children require you to become less selfish and suddenly someone else's life is as important as your own.

Having a child is one of the greatest experiences life can offer us and the unconditional love a parent feels is something you cannot understand until you have a child of your own. Careers, holidays and friends may change with a baby, but this does not mean they have to become unrewarding. I had no intentions whatsoever of having a baby until I became accidentally pregnant, but I would not go back now even though my pregnancies were difficult. In fact, I chose to have a second.

At the end of one's life no one will look back and say 'I wish I'd spent more time at the office' or 'I wish I'd had one more holiday'. A child will truly leave a little bit of you in the world and can there be a more haunting regret than 'I wish I'd had children'?

Mrs L Nutter, Lancashire

Chapter 4
Instinct and Reason

Subdue your appetites, my dears, and you've conquered human nature.
Charles Dickens

Parents still talk about *when our children arrived*, as though they came home from the shops on a typically dull Thursday to find a 'while you were out' card from Fedex on the doormat. It's understandable how problems can arise further down the line when they discover how the contents of the parcel impedes upon their lives.

In 2003, *Good Housekeeping* magazine commissioned a survey asking mothers about the impact of having children.[1] The results were as follows:

Damaged my career 90%
Damaged my family life 61%

Caused lost friendships 60%
Damaged my sex life 50%
Led to separation or divorce 12%

Our survey paints a devastating picture of a woman so drained of her resources that all her vital relationships are in danger. It helps explain exactly why the birth rate is plummeting.

Editor, Good Housekeeping, 2003

Everyone asks 'Why don't you have children?' Nobody asks parents 'Why do you have children?' which is an equally good question in modern times. Childfree North Americans might call it a no-brainer. Put starkly, *why* would a person choose the regimented conformity, worry and potential penury that children involve over a life of fun and freedom?

Childfree people have weighed up the pros and cons of having a family and made their choice based on practicalities and the type of lifestyle they'd prefer. Although they shouldn't have to, they can justify their choice because they've arrived there cerebrally. On the rare occasions parents are asked why they became parents however, most are flummoxed. A popular reason is that they answered an innate 'biological urge' or 'maternal instinct', over which they had little control.

I've been broody since I was 16. I can remember the moment – I was working in my summer job, selling school uniforms. A mother came in with her children, and while her son was trying the uniform on she asked me to hold her baby. With him there in my

> arms I felt this sudden, massive warmth. Later at university, when asked what I wanted to be I said 'a mum'. The right circumstances haven't happened yet, but I will consider IVF or adoption if I need to.
>
> *Isobel, 34, marketing manager*

But plenty of women have strong nurturing instincts and have experienced the same feeling Isobel describes without it transferring into a need to have a child. Somewhere along the line rationality kicked in and a realisation that motherhood is not all about those contented moments overrode what we commonly call maternal instinct. It's complex because the word 'instinct' is used in many senses. Childfree people might also say that they 'trusted their instincts' when deciding not to have children.

As long ago as 1924, the American psychologist Luther Lee Bernard noted that the blanket term 'instinct' was being used misleadingly in regard to motherhood.[2] 'This so called "tender" emotion,' he wrote, 'is not instinctive or inherited. Children are busy in their early years with imitating their elders in all conceivable practices. It is an acquired emotional attitude.' Modern analysts, too, refer to the word as a metaphor. Some people evidently feel more warmth toward children than others. But whether or not it's built into our make-up, or absorbed subconsciously is part of the debate on nature and nurture that has been raging for decades.

Bernard extends his theory to men, writing:

> **... it will be even more readily apparent that we are not justified in speaking of a paternal instinct ...**

> **[The father] has been induced to become interested in his offspring in comparatively recent times through the growth of humanitarian sentiment and tradition in society at large, which has built up a cult about the child and has gradually drawn the male parent also into its circle to worship at its altar.**

(Men's attitude to parenting is further discussed in chapter 8.)

Some people turn to the animal kingdom to explain what they mean when they talk of the 'biological urge' that caused them to have children. The strength of evolutionary programming is certainly very evident there. Some spiders are so intent on spreading their genes that the male allows himself to be eaten by the female during copulation. He even turns his head towards her head, so she can munch through most of his body, leaving his busy genitals until last. The theory is that a well-nourished female spider will make more eggs and thus produce more babies; ultimate self-sacrifice for the greater good of species survival. (These particular spiders live in parts of the world where meeting a mate in the undergrowth is harder than it is in London, so the option of the male simply moving on to fertilise more females is remote.)

Among mammal and bird species the need to spread genes is likewise innate, though the outcome for the males is less terminal than for arthropods. But the outstanding difference that separates man from beast is that humans can think and make rational decisions in a way that animals can't.

I want to be sterilised to assert the supremacy of mind over body. People are shocked. I'm at Cambridge and the other students say 'what if you change your mind?' But what if someone had a baby and changed their mind? That, I would imagine, would have far more complications. My doctor won't refer me until I'm 21. She is afraid that I'll change my mind and sue her. She has absolutely nothing to worry about, of course. One cannot have an intelligent conversation with children and I don't find them remotely pleasant to look at. They are uncoordinated and irritating. People say I might love a baby if it was mine, but to love something without just cause would corrupt my reason and purpose of life. It wouldn't be flattering to be loved by a baby who knows no better and I won't be a slave to anybody for the sake of love. Just as one does not give money to people except in exchange for goods, so one does not give one's love, friendship or esteem except in exchange for virtues that are worthy of these values. I have Asberger's syndrome, which runs in my family, and we also have a family history of Alzheimer's and Parkinson's disease. The chances are I would pass on these revolting conditions and I wouldn't want to do that. I am also prone to depression and try to avoid the causes thereof. Post-natal depression affects many women so it's not worth it for me. My immediate ancestors are awful about my decision because they want grandchildren, but since I hate them anyway it doesn't

> matter – they'd never see them. They've moved on to pester my younger sister instead; she likes children but doesn't want any of her own. My aunt is sometimes honest about the stress she is under with her three awful triplets. As soon as I am able I will follow Philip Larkin's advice. Life is about taking responsibility for oneself. Most people are bad at it. I love being childfree. Those moments when you know you are not answerable to anyone and can go out and enjoy yourself as you please make any social event twice as thrilling.
>
> *Pippa, 19, student of French and Russian*

Empirically, it seems, there is no common thread when it comes to family experience influencing a desire to procreate. Those who grew up in large families sometimes continue the pattern, and sometimes react against it and remain childfree. Those without brothers and sisters may not like the thought of being surrounded by boisterous children of their own, or they may have lots, because they craved company when they were small.

It could be that our individual genes are responsible for making some of us more needy of, or better at, motherhood than others. Scientific progress has spawned reports that genes might make us fast runners, criminals or mathematical geniuses, but the science itself is still in its infancy.

We don't know if some women are genetically preconditioned to want to reproduce more than others. The media likes catchy headlines and we've seen

plenty of them in the field of genetics. It's in fact very dangerous to suggest that there's a 'gene for this' and a 'gene for that'. It's very complex. But what you read about 'criminal genes' or 'good-at-maths genes' is at least rooted in science. The question people really want answered is not a scientific one, but one about differences in ability and actions. To use crime as an example: someone with schizophrenia may hear voices in his head that tell him to do something criminal, like push someone in front of a train. The schizophrenia has a genetic component, but the criminal act does not. Of course women have maternal genes – genes that give them breasts and ovaries and enable them to be mothers. But we don't know if some have genes that make them want motherhood more or will make them better at it. Billions of dollars has been spent on research and development in agriculture to see which cattle produce the most milk, thus making high returns for the farmer. A cow with a high milk yield is a good mother-cow and scientists have found genes that contribute to high milk production. Tests have also been done on rats and their babies. If an upset is caused among new mother-rats, some will pick up their babies before running away and others will just run away. Again that suggests that genetics play a part. But nothing is proven.

Steve Jones, professor in genetics, University College London

It's not uncommon for animals to turn viciously on their young and even the most patient human mother will tell you that her 'maternal instinct' frays when the children refuse to go to sleep or the baby won't stop crying. It would be reasonable to suppose that those who want to become parents have considered the degree to which they believe the joys will outweigh the demands, and felt confident in their own levels of tolerance to go ahead. But mostly it's not the case.

> **Our conversations with parents revealed a certain antipathy to the very idea of 'choice'. Women spoke about 'finding that they were pregnant' either as the result of an accident or because they or their partner had somehow become casual about contraception. But even this 'casualness' was a complicated business. In some cases it sounded like nothing but carelessness; in others it seemed to be based on a tacit acceptance that if pregnancy occurred as a result of this casualness, then nature should be allowed 'to take its course'.**
>
> *From* What Are Children For? *by Laurie Taylor and Matthew Taylor*

When friction between mothers and childfree women arises it's possibly because mothers dislike confronting the fact that they didn't think very hard about a decision that can be as problematical as it can be rewarding. Mothers and non-mothers are becoming ever more polarised. Any group of young women discovering careers, friends and financial independence will tell you they're having the time of their lives.

Women love the modern privilege of self-discovery and it's become available to high numbers of us. As a result, more of us are choosing not to have children at all. But in contrast and at the same time there's a frenzied drive among many women in their late thirties and early forties to get pregnant at a time when nature can disappoint. Some women will be in this situation through circumstance, but even those in stable couples are postponing pregnancy precisely because they're enjoying pursuing their own goals. So why do they have children?

One of my friends who wants kids told me: 'If you don't have a baby it's like being refused entry to an exclusive club.' It made her want to join, it made me want to gag.

Is it that female hormones scream loudest when time is running out, or could it be that social pressure is as much responsible for a sudden desire to chuck in an enjoyable life for the sum of a baby's parts?

'Life is not just about having babies,' said the head of the UK's fertility regulator the HFEA when she was appointed.[3] 'Don't be panicked into starting a family by the ticking of your biological clock.' But Suzi Leather is competing with the roar of media, advertising, child crazy mothers and family friendly governments. Parenthood is a big, bright bandwagon, and Babylust is causing hysteria in the queue for tickets at the bus stop.

There might indeed be a biological time limit upon women's capacity to reproduce but that is not the same thing as saying that they are genetically predetermined to breed. What we are really talking about here is not an instinct but purely cultural fear and

anxiety, the fear of being left behind, the fear of not fitting in with all your friends who have children, the fear of growing old and being lonely, the fear that your partner will leave you if you never have children ... Our decisions about whether to have children or remain childfree are heavily influenced by our anticipation of how others will view our choices.

From What Are Children For? *by Laurie Taylor and Matthew Taylor*

Everyone around me was having children. My older sister had two by the time I got married and my brother had a baby a year later. I never had the urge to have children. I've always been different to my sister and brother in my outlook on life. But I felt everyone was waiting for me to get pregnant and it might sound silly but I didn't want to disappoint. I love my children – I had two – but I couldn't say I've enjoyed being a mother and I'm not sure I've been very good at it. My husband and I divorced when the children were small. I still love him and I wonder whether we might be together if we'd had more time for each other. If not having kids had been more acceptable I'd have said 'no thanks'.

Tracey, 50, Liverpool

While Charles Darwin was writing *The Origin of Species* in the mid-19th century he hid the manuscript for fear of the immense controversy it would create in a God-fearing nation. Today, it's equally controversial to suggest that social factors and pressure to conform are a greater influence in a decision to have a baby than biology. Modern women like to be thought of as independent and free thinking after all.

Advertisers (aka the Want Makers) play a big part in influencing people to conform through material aspiration. In the luxury goods market they use images that tell us money and a smart job are what's needed to gain access to the in-crowd. Another proven method of enticement to spend is the portrayal of family life as a mark of success.

An advert for toilet roll implies that ingredients for a happy life include a toddler, a puppy and a sparkly bathroom in a big house. In reality of course these things have nothing to do with toilet roll and little to do with happiness. There are hundreds of examples. Day to day products (food, washing powder) and expensive products (cars, holidays, insurance policies) use children in their marketing strategies to great effect. I've even seen an air-freshener called 'Bébé'. Rather than the usual 'alpine' or 'floral' scent, this one promises: 'Now every corner of your home can smell like your baby'. A mixed blessing in reality, one might have thought. When advertising campaigns are successful, the notion is reinforced that those who don't want or can't afford a current trend are living on the fringes of society. You may feel excluded because you don't have a smart car or an iPod or because you can't afford luxury toilet roll. But the picture is so blurred that you may feel excluded because you don't have money, a job, or a baby. Sometimes it seems like the whole glossy package of parenthood is for sale rather than the particular product being advertised. Increasingly in our society, anything to do with children is considered joyous, amusing

more than a cosy panacea wrapped in double standards, because if anyone dared to suggest women are governed by their hormones in any other capacity, she'd probably be the first to be outraged. Usually, women don't like to be judged by their gender. Most of us over about 30 will remember an unenlightened male boss at some point in their working lives resorting to the 'she's got PMT' strategy when faced with an assertive female in the office. It was damning, yet the hormonal 'maternal desire' is accepted with universal placidity because it has tradition on its side. Childfree women don't have the riot-shield equivalent of a 'biological urge' to hide behind, and for some reason, saying that we thought carefully about our decision is seen as a bad thing!

Parents who find themselves ground down by the demands of their kids must feel they don't have a leg to stand on if their reasons for having them are questioned.

It's also possible that some people opt for, or fall into parenthood because it's easier than thinking what else to do or because it shields them from living on their own. A guaranteed busy schedule is quite literally delivered into the arms of new parents, which suits a lot of people well. Being childfree has numerous advantages, but it does require motivation – you need to find fulfilling stuff to do, which comes more easily to some than others. Women never have to justify their lives once they've had a baby and they often don't have to earn a living – at least if there's a man in the house. Recent research shows that in the UK, men are still the breadwinners in 91 per cent of cases.[4] Painting your own life on a blank canvas is equally challenging as dealing with the incessant needs of children, but arguably more rewarding.

> Everyone has a need to be loved and wanted. If you're lucky, that's provided by a partner. But many women are insecure in their relationships. They're not 100 per cent confident their man loves them, but a baby fills the emptiness, loves and needs them without question and, in some cases, keeps them their man as well. That's how it is for me. My husband has never treated me well – he is cold towards me and has affairs with other women. But I have a beautiful home, a car and a good lifestyle and my children are my reward for putting up with him. He would leave me, but he would not gain custody of his children and he wouldn't leave them.
>
> *Miriam, 50, mother of two*

Not all women are empowered of course, or feel they want to be. Once on a bus, shortly after a widely reported sexual attack on a small girl, I overheard one lady say to another, 'I can't understand paedophiles, and I can't understand women who don't want children either' – as though it were appropriate to bracket the two together. In another confusing twist, some are offended by the notion that having a baby could be influenced by anything *other* than an innate desire or, interestingly, a higher calling. A friend who's a Catholic priest mentioned that he felt fed up with people telling him what a wonderful 'real father' he'd make. He acknowledged however that the comments were always warm or jovial – his vocation and celibacy were accepted if not understood – whereas childfree women are condemned as cold-hearted. It's an allegation that's particularly annoying because many, in an exceptionally compassionate sense, are shying away from the emotional implications of bringing a vulnerable new person into a troubled world, unconsulted and on their own whim. Feeling helpless in the face of a child's unhappiness would be a lot to bear – the best compensation you can offer attached to a Woolworth's label. Compared to 1974 figures, today's fifteen year olds are more than twice as likely to display behavioural problems such as lying, stealing and disobedience, and are 70 per cent more likely to experience anxiety and depression.[5] Some non-parents are doing pain avoidance on a large scale.

> I am scared of my youngest child and I am scared for him. He has behavioural problems but the doctor can't make a specific diagnosis – he is just a very troubled little boy. Sometimes he is physically violent and he will scream and cry with rage for no apparent reason. I feel a terrible guilt that I have done something wrong in the way I have brought him up and that nothing I do calms him down. The strain on our marriage is unbearable. It is terrible to know that you have created a little human being who is so ill at ease with the world.
>
> *Mary, 33, north of England*

> I'm a happy person myself, but I find it hard to reconcile the uncertainty of the future with childrearing. My own reasons might be construed as dramatic, but they're valid. I grew up in Dover where my dad was editor of the local newspaper. A watershed time for me

was 1987 when I was 13. *The Herald of Free Enterprise*, a passenger ferry crossing to Zeebrugge in Belgium, capsized with the loss of 192 lives. Everyone in Dover knew someone who worked on the boats or at the docks – three of my classmates lost their fathers in the accident. My family and I were on holiday in France and had to come home early because of how it impacted on my dad's job. I can remember waving him off in a helicopter to take the now world-famous photo of the ship lying on its side in the middle of the English Channel. Dover never really recovered. It was at this time, which coincided with the onset of adolescence that I really started to worry about the world. Similar tragedies in later years (the massacre of schoolchildren at Dunblane in Scotland, for example) have made me think that I don't want to bring children into this world. Obviously I comprehend that what happened to [child murder victims] Holly Wells, Jessica Chapman and Milly Dowler is very rare, but when you've tasted the pain of human tragedy, you come nearer to knowing the heartbreak. The sinking of the *Herald* was tangible for me and I think differently about the world because of it. The risk of anything happening to children that I had brought into the world – the fear and worry for them – outweighs the considerable possibility that they'd outlive me. But I'm not prepared to take the gamble. The world is not a good enough place for children, there is too much instability.

Jessica, 29, radio producer, London

Laurie Hubbs
PhD Thesis: The Differences Between Parents, Childfree and Childless People in North America
b 1958

Working as a therapist I came to realise that issues surrounding children – in one way or another – were at the centre of the majority of my patients' problems. It interested me so I decided to do my PhD research on this topic – attitudes towards childlessness in the United States. The unhappiness people feel about child-related issues covers the three categories into which I divided the research. It seems to me that in relation to procreation nobody wins, regardless of the category they are in. Many parents are miserable because of their relationships with their children; many childfree people suffer because of pressures and hostile reactions; childless people are upset because they can't have a baby. I also have patients in a couple, where there is tension because one wants to have children and the other doesn't.

I describe myself as childfree, but I made the transition from being childless. A medical condition meant that having a baby was not a possibility for me. There was no ambiguity and no possibility of fertility treatment, so my husband and I decided to make a mental adjustment and get on with our lives. I expect that we are missing something by not having children, but it's not possible to do everything in life, so we are all missing out on some things! The point is, I am happy with my life and not having children has given my husband and I remarkable freedom to pursue things that are important to us. We have lots of children in our lives. We love our nieces and nephews and have great relationships with them. We enjoy our friends' children. We just don't feel the need to have any of our own.

The whole issue of parenthood and non-parenthood is very complex. I have been amazed at the intensity of responses I have received when I talk about my dissertation topic. It appears to me that parents, especially mothers, react as though I am committing a mortal sin with the mere suggestion that it is okay to not have children. Even suggesting that having children is a choice often meets with an aggressive response. The other side of the spectrum is represented by people who are relieved to find someone who does not view their childfree status as a negative.

Much of my research focuses on 'social desirability'. It's evident that a majority of people still have a desire to conform to a social norm and I wonder if this desire is more prevalent among parents and childless people. I think normalcy is greatly overrated.

I suspect that many people do not think about having children – anyone can do it and they have them by default because society expects them to. The moment someone gets married friends and family begin asking, 'When are you starting a family?' Many couples have children by a timescale. If they have been married for two years, it's time to get pregnant. They do not consider 'will we be capable parents?' or 'is this what we would like to do?' And because this is the way things are, nobody has to make a decision or accept responsibility for becoming a parent. They can just say, 'Oh, it's part of life, it happened to me, I had no choice'. I think this is indicative of our need for social bonding. Social bonding is important to people – we need it. In history, it was key to survival – people lived close to each other, in clans or groups to provide mutual protection and livelihood. Now it isn't necessary for survival but it is important for emotional well-being.

I am sceptical of the 'biological urge', because if it is innate in humankind, why is it that a significantly

increasing number of women are not having babies? There are tragic flaws in the way biological ties are considered superior to any others. Frequently in my clinical work I have distressed people saying to me, 'I'm a lousy parent, I wish I had never done it.' Parenting is such an important job and parents should be valued for the work they are doing. However, the well-being of children has far reaching consequences for all of society, so if an individual is not interested, or does not want to be a parent, their decision must be respected too.

What I am really struggling with right now is why this is such a volatile subject. What is it about the issue of procreation that evokes such strong reactions? Any ideas? It puzzles me that in these 'live and let live' times our attitudes still seem stuck in the mindset that everyone must do the same thing. My research is new, there needs to be a lot more in this very important field.

Chapter 5
Consumerism

Man is the only animal whose desires increase as they are fed; the only animal that is never satisfied.
Henry George

Couples often explain that they had a first baby to 'complete their happiness' or because 'something was missing'. The vast majority of childfree people don't feel that something is lacking in their lives, at least not on the scale that needs filling by a baby. If you're not content without a baby, it's unlikely a baby will make you content. And if you are content, why have a baby?

Perhaps you're content, but want to be more content? Dissatisfaction is recognised as an innate component of the human condition. Buddhists might say that always wanting more arises from spiritual ignorance, Christians that it's evidence of original sin. Evolutionary psychologists take the view that incessant craving is inherent in Darwinian philosophy - the caveman with an urge to impregnate as many women as possible would have done more to ensure the survival of his species than the one who slept on his lion rug all day. But natural impulses that served us well in Stone Age times no longer do so. In the modern world the conditions that confer reproductive advantages are not the same conditions that confer peace and happiness.

> **'The Beautiful Frock', Edward Monkton**
> **'Buy me, Lady', said the frock,**
> **'and I will make you into a**
> **BEAUTIFUL and WHOLE and**
> **COMPLETE Human Being.'**
> **'Do not be SILLY, said the Man,**
> **'for a frock alone cannot do that.'**
> **'TRUE, said the Lady. 'I will**
> **have the Shoes and the Bag as well.'**

It might seem churlish to compare an item of clothing to a flesh and blood baby, except that the so-called 'designer baby' market is thriving, particularly in America, and most people acknowledge that not everyone who has children has the means or the inclination to care for them properly. 'Accessory babies' have become a visible extension of the consumer cultures of affluent nations. Accessory babies need ... well, accessories, and so do their parents. Immediately post conception, mothers are enticed into the multi-million pound baby-product market.

There are no gaps in this market. Preggie Pops (childfree women will know them as fruit flavoured lollies) can help combat queasiness from day one and, towards the end of the nine-month adventure, why not have a belly cast made in plaster of Paris to remind you (should you care to be reminded) of the shape of your body before you gave birth. The sales pitch assures that the finished product combines beauty with practicality and can be used to decorate the home as an uplighter or a large receptacle for pot pourri.

Prince Charles apparently rolls up his depleting toothpaste tubes with a solid platinum stick commissioned exclusively for the purpose. Many of the must-have baby products on sale are equally superfluous and evidently satisfy a craving within the parent rather than the child. There are expensive alpaca kick rugs (which I bet are dry-clean only) and solid silver containers for the tooth fairy. In my limited experience, a blanket and an empty matchbox would please most infants as much. In America, the Mosaic Heirloom Princess Bed from Posh Tots will set you back $2,190 (appx £1,200). (But with it, 'your house can feel like a museum gallery,' so perhaps it is worthwhile.)

It's tempting to conclude that we live in a child-centred society, but try telling that to one of the many rejected or abused children we live alongside. The notion would seem bewildering.

> I think vanity has a lot to do with wanting children and I must admit I would be curious to see what a little version of me looked like. I'm gay and it wouldn't be impossible, but it's not a very sound reason for being a parent is it? A few years ago, travelling in Uganda, I visited an orphanage. Two staff were trying to cope with about 40 children. They had no time to cuddle them, they just fed them, washed them and put them back in

> their little iron cots. Scraps of paper were pinned overhead with each child's story written on them: 'Moses, aged six months, found on the steps of the mortuary', 'Gloria, four months, found at the rubbish dump with another baby who has died'. A small boy took a shine to me and it was the first time I felt a real emotional pull towards a child. He had never known affection. I looked into offering him a home because I knew I could make such a difference to his life, but for lots of reasons it didn't work out. I bought a washing machine for the orphanage. It wasn't much and I still feel emotional when I think of that boy. He'll be about seven now, squatting, probably naked, on the side of the road, trying to sell un-saleable things like gravel or old bits of fruit. When you see the crushing poverty in some parts of the world it's hard to feel good about how children in rich nations are given so much.
>
> *Rob, 42, London*

In China (where the written symbol for 'choice' is the same as it is for 'confusion') many small children don't wear nappies – their trousers and romper suits are designed with no bottoms. Western parents might question the efficacy of the system, but it works for the Chinese and is entirely acceptable because all parents dress their kids the same way. The supermarkets of wealthy nations meanwhile are stacked high with competing brands of nappies for every occasion. Alongside them are hundreds of baby oils and potions that many doctors believe are responsible for a rise in previously unheard of skin conditions and allergies.

Freedom of choice may be of fundamental importance for the big issues in life (whether women have children, for example), but when it's thrust upon you in copious quantities, it's as overwhelming as trying to buy a sandwich in a New York deli.

All of us have been victims of consumerism since the day we were born and there are no signs that our enthusiasm for all things material is doing anything other than intensifying. Youngsters rate shopping their number one 'hobby' and in the UK the Swedish furniture store IKEA is the modern church – it flings open its doors on a Sunday morning and the congregation of customers flocks in. But it's children who represent more market potential than any other demographic segment because they have a powerful influence over their parents' buying decisions and hold great promise as future adult consumers. In our quick-fix culture, where gratification can be purchased and time is short, parents face an uphill struggle in teaching their kids humane values.

A friend whose two girls are in fee paying schools was amazed when I idly wondered if teacher still gets an apple on the last day of term. 'An apple!' she laughed, wide-eyed. 'At Easter it was a Hermes scarf and at Christmas it's a hamper!'

In the UK, among eight to sixteen year olds:

86% have a television in their bedroom.

82% have their own music system.

A quarter have a computer.[1]

25% of children aged seven to ten own mobile phones – with primary school children aged five upwards the fastest growing market.[2]

Although the industry claims not to target children, Winnie-the-Pooh, Spiderman and Barbie handsets are widely available. Thousands of pounds per family are spent on designer clothes and sports equipment in the youth market. Meanwhile, a US report shows parents spend ten to fifteen hours less per week with their children than they did in the 1960s,[3] and teachers in the UK tell of children beginning their school lives with such poor skills that they can't hold a crayon let alone a knife and fork and have never eaten a meal at a table. While plenty want for nothing in the material stakes, one in three children in Britain (3.8 million families) lives below the poverty line.[4] The prospect of being dragged into a world of conspicuous consumerism can contribute to a decision to remain childfree. It's a relief to bypass the daily humdrum of family life and while many issues warrant effort of thought, whether it's fair that next-door-has-a-trampoline-and-we-don't isn't one of them.

> Children grind you down. The permanent 'I want, I want, I want,' is exhausting. When they moan 'I'm bored,' I sometimes shout back at them, 'And you think I'm not?' I never know if buying them the latest craze is the right thing to do, but if I don't I feel guilty they're missing out on something all the other kids have got. Usually it's some bit of expensive plastic that's yesterday's news by the end of the week. Children can be very manipulative – they tell you they'll be bullied at school if you don't buy them something that they want.
>
> *Penny, Lancashire*

> I have heard people say 'you've got to give kids what they want these days', although this seems to mean spending money on them, not time, love or attention. I remember a woman cutting my hair talking about hiring a stretch limo for her kids to go to a school disco and how expensive it was. I wanted to tell her to put them on the bus! I wouldn't want to be a child now, or the parent of a child. The peer pressure was bad enough in my day but the world seems so conformist now, you either fit in or you don't. Everyone is so concerned about how they look. I was always climbing trees and jumping in streams. I think children everywhere have the potential to be charming little people, but most of the ones I encounter just whine all the time.
>
> *Glenda, South Wales*

American scientist Dimitri Christakis who carried out research from his base at Seattle Children's Hospital would like to see a ban on television for all children under two. His report into Attention Deficit Disorders[5] found that every hour of television watched by toddlers caused a ten per cent increased risk of developing concentration problems by age seven. His theory is that television over-stimulates the young brain with unrealistically fast-paced images (cartoons, for example) that may permanently 're-wire' the connections within it, causing restlessness, impulsiveness and confusion.

According to a survey by the UK's *Mother & Baby* magazine,[6] children under three routinely spend up to five hours a day staring at a TV screen. The research, which looked at hot-housing and behavioural trends, questioned children as well as adults. The youngest participants, rather than appreciating the methods used most often to keep them occupied, unanimously agreed that their favourite pastimes are 'going to the park' and 'visiting grandma'.

How We Are Ruining Our Children

There is a climate of fear that surrounds parenting today. People panic, assuming that they don't know what they are doing, but the conflicting views of 'experts' – many of whom are too old to remember their own experiences as parents – don't help. Children arrive like unexploded bombs and there is an enormous pressure not to make mistakes. As my mother used to say, 'It all goes wrong in the labour rooms'. In other words, one slip with the forceps and he fails his maths GCSE.

The tendency to overindulge is understandable. In many families now, both parents work full-time and are with their children so briefly every day that their attitudes are conditioned by a sense of guilt. They feel that in order to provide for their children they are also abandoning them, so they shy away from confrontation in the one or two hours a day that they spend together.

But the constant refrain from frustrated parents of 'What can I do?' drives me mad. Parenting is difficult, but if your children watch too much TV, it's no use denying your own responsibility. I never allowed my children to turn on a television at least until

Thomas the Tank Engine came on in the afternoon – breakfast TV simply was not allowed. I think they accepted this rationing because I stated firmly that this was how things were and there was no use arguing about it. There was no need to be aggressive: I found that as long as I was confident I was doing the right thing, it was possible to set the boundaries and maintain a relaxed, happy relationship with my children. Parents argue that their children are unhappy if they haven't seen the latest episode of whatever it is that all their friends are watching, and so they 'have no choice' but to let them watch it.

This is a nonsense brought about by a complete lack of proportion. Ask them later in life if missing _Scooby-Doo_ really blighted their lives: the answer will be no.

Libby Purves, broadcaster, from* The Times, *6 April 2004

One in ten young people has attempted suicide in the UK according to the youth charity Young Voice.[7] A fifth of those questioned said pressure from school work and peers is 'unbearably high', but they rarely turned to their parents for support because they're often too stressed or exhausted themselves to help. Cases of self-harm among teenagers, particularly girls aged 11 to 15, all but doubled in a six-year period in the 1990s.[8] New Zealand, Canada and Australia have among the highest record of youth suicides among industrialised nations[9] and images of school shootings in America have shocked the world in recent years. Doctors warn that the present generation of teenagers will turn into the most obese and unhealthy adults in the history of mankind.

Certain topics surrounding parenthood have become highly politicised – with those in different camps staging the same determined stand offs as serial mothers against the seriously childfree. Whether it's best to work full-time, stay at home, employ a nanny, go for state education or pay boarding school fees are topics for heated debate, though I can think of examples of all these options working well for different families. Having a child is easier than adopting a pet from Battersea Dog's Home. The common necessity is surely that those who choose to become parents feel in a position to offer wholehearted and consistent commitment to the welfare and upbringing of the children they choose to bring into the world. How many they have and how they arrange their personal circumstances is bound to differ.

There was an old woman who lived in a shoe.
She had so many children,
She didn't know what to do.
She gave them some broth,
Without any bread,
Whipped them all soundly,
And sent them to bed.

Childfree people often say that their decision was based on the realisation that they lacked the time, desire or motivation required to be a good parent which, rather than being interpreted negatively, could be admired.

Rachel Cusk
writer
b 1967

A Life's Work: On Becoming A Mother (Fourth Estate)

Rachel Cusk's honest account of motherhood for the first year of her daughter's life caused an indignant outcry when it was first published. She was vilified by mothers who must have felt she'd 'spilled the beans' on what looking after a baby can really be like. She shares her feelings of resentment with candid appeal – and reveals the living hell of sitting in a circle singing 'The Wheels on the Bus Go Round and Round' over and over again.

I was preoccupied with whether I'd have children even when I was a child myself. I believe in exploring the human condition and experiencing every available state – so pregnancy, childbirth and motherhood were almost inevitable for me. I worried about it, but I never felt strongly against having children.

Becoming a mother is an unbelievable shock. When you've grown up a feminist it erodes your self-esteem. You're suddenly expected to morph into a low-status, boring, relentlessly demanding, exhausting role. I often think people wouldn't have children if they knew what it was like.

You become public property from the moment you get pregnant. Doctors call you 'mother' and strangers think it's ok to reach out and rub your tummy.

> ***Motherhood is a demotion. My relish for it approximates that of the average filing clerk.***

I remember being wheeled back from the delivery room, cradling my new daughter in my arms. The midwife suggested she might like a feed. It didn't feel natural to me – it felt as though I was being pushed along a hospital corridor in full view of everyone as somebody sucked my breast.

Most of all I remember the dawning realisation that although I'd just produced a baby and was exhausted and emotional, I wasn't going to be a priority, ever again in my life.

Family life is fundamentally flawed – unbearable, awful and insufferable are the words I used in the book. Months after I gave birth I still really missed being able to do simple things like sleep-in or spend a Saturday morning reading a book. I missed the spontaneity I'd been so accustomed to – popping out for a walk, going swimming or wandering down to the pub for a drink.

> ***The loss of these things seemed a high, an exorbitant price to pay for the privilege of motherhood.***

I also discovered how motherhood attracts desperate sexism and conservatism. In my community now a popular first question is 'what does your husband do?' We wouldn't have moved away from London if we hadn't had children. Picking up from playgroup is a part of the day I hate, but for once recently I overheard something that sounded quite interesting and tried to join in. The mothers were talking about how to download information from the internet so I edged closer. Within minutes I found myself stuck in a conversation about a treatment for nits! I mean, what are these women's lives about? Another time, a woman piped up that her daughter bursts into tears when she sees a black person because she's frightened of black people. The other mothers just laughed, but that sort of thing is not uncommon and it's mind-numbing.

> *The hardship of parenthood is so unrelievedly shocking. At its worst moments it does indeed resemble hell, in the sense that its torments are never ending, that its drama is conducted in full view of the heaven of freedom.*

I had a surprise second baby soon after my first. I'm pleased because if I'd had to think about it, it would have taken me five or six years to contemplate going through it again. In the UK we're used to enjoying a lifestyle that's unheard of in other cultures. It makes motherhood all the more shocking. I think most people are broken by it, in reality.

> *When I look through old photographs of myself it's like looking at the ruins of Pompeii ... Motherhood is an exercise in conformity from which no amount of subterfuge can liberate the soul ...*

Chapter 6
Environment and Population

Somewhere on this globe, every three seconds, there is a woman giving birth to a child. She must be found and stopped.
Sam Levenson

Whether environmental reasons feature towards the top or the bottom of their list, most contented non-parents feel that there are plenty of people in the world already. They share the eminent company of naturalist David Attenborough, physicist Steven Hawking and environmentalist Jonathan Porritt to name a few, who are so concerned about the consequences of population growth that they want to see state-led policies that promote smaller families and offer financial incentives to women who remain childfree.

Spain has the lowest birth rate in the world (excluding China) and Yemen the highest.

Average number of children per woman

Yemen 7.6
Spain 1.1

South Africa 2.8
US 2.1
Ireland 2.0
New Zealand 1.9
Australia 1.7
UK 1.6
Canada 1.5[1]

Jewish women across Israel have an average 2.6 children each, but in Israeli settlements the figure rises to 4.7. Palestinian women have an average 5.7 children each – a reflection of the motivation behind fertility in unstable parts of the world. In these extremes a political and religious imperative to populate the land is at work, although many couples living in peaceful countries also talk of a need to leave a footprint on the world.

In Greece, there's been a notable trend in the last few years towards women having only one child – perhaps to remain just the right side of what's culturally acceptable.

Falling birth rates in western countries make it easy for people to reproduce without engaging their conscience. The very few who are environmentally aware enough to even consider the problems of population growth can convince themselves that having more babies is okay, because the birth rate where they live is low. But over-population is a problem everywhere, not just in the developing world. To highlight South Africa as an example: The birth rate, in keeping with western trends, has fallen significantly in recent years. The death rate is high because of AIDS. But the population still rises rapidly, because even with a low birth rate and a high death rate – more people are being born than are dying. Governments in richer nations, however, concentrate on increasing support for people who choose to have children. There are tax breaks and family friendly workplace policies, and even campaigns that encourage large families with slogans like 'Avoid a Birth Dearth!' The UK Conservative party encouraged women to 'Breed for Britain'[2] and Australia's Family First Party supports 'decisive action to reverse declining trends in the birth rate'.[3]

Most people (world leaders and media gurus included) have children, so it's not surprising that the economic argument for increasing the birth rate is more common than the less heard *environmental* point of view that supports population reduction.

> **My biggest worry is population growth, and if it continues at the current rate, we will be standing shoulder to shoulder in 2600. Something has to be done, and I don't want it to be a disaster.**
>
> ***Stephen Hawking, theoretical physicist,***
> ***author* A Brief History of Time**[4]

Environmentalists adhere to a 'less is more' philosophy while economics students are taught that 'more makes more' (perpetual economic motion). Governments say they need to keep population levels up to safeguard the economy, but in 2003, sparsely populated Finland (which produced Nokia, one of the world's largest companies) was rated highest for growth prospects.[5] Elder care and health facilities, not to mention state pensions, are costly in countries where the population is ageing rapidly. Families are encouraged on the basis that an increase in young people will translate into support for the old people. The theory seems contrived and short-sighted to environmentalists because people of all ages take from the state – and what happens when the young people grow old themselves? Those who promote the policy must either believe that the world can sustain infinite numbers of people (environmentalists say it can't), or they don't care what happens a few generations down the line because they'll be out of the picture.

In the UK, no-one who's walked through city streets, joined a waiting list for health care, commuted by train, sat in traffic or sought education for their child in a class of fewer than 30 can seriously pretend that over-crowding isn't an issue. Inner city doctors are reporting significant rises in tuberculosis,[6] another implication of too high a population density, and there are very few places remote enough to stand alone and hear only natural sound.

China's One Child Initiative is the only state-imposed population control measure in the world. Under it, urban families who produce more than one child can be penalised financially, ostracised socially and in some cases even imprisoned. Such methods are entirely unacceptable to western ways of thinking because of the human rights implications. There are terrible reports of female foetuses being aborted in high numbers and female infanticide because boys are favoured in Chinese culture. But incentives not to have children rather than punishments for having them could be an acceptable means of achieving similar results. An estimated 300 million births have been prevented in China since the one-child policy was introduced in 1980 and a country prone to floods and famine is now largely able to feed and educate its population.[7]

Existing human resources could be better distributed around the globe, but that's also too sensitive a notion to gain attention on the political stage. Immigration is deeply unpopular and people from overseas are often blamed for difficulties that arise as a result of high population density in their new country. The idea of a big, happy melting pot appeals only to a progressive minority. The same politicians who urge their indigenous women to have more children can also be heard calling for a reduction in immigrant numbers.

1930 – 2 billion people in the world
1980 – 4 billion people in the world
1999 – 6 billion people in the world[8]

To mark the millennium, ABC television's *Nightline* (a similar programme to the UK's Newsnight) ran a two-part programme about life in the future.[9] CIA analysts predicted that by 2015 over-population will detrimentally affect everyone worldwide, the USA included. But the idea that population growth could be voluntarily curbed was dismissed.

> **Instead of controlling the environment for the benefit of the population, maybe we should control the population to ensure the survival of the environment.**
>
> ***David Attenborough, naturalist, broadcaster and writer***[10]

Thailand holds a Free Sterilisation Day on the king's birthday each year and many Indian states have population planning incentives, though some veer towards the unusual. In Uttar Pradesh, anyone applying for a gun permit must either invest 50,000 rupees, or appear at a state-run health centre with five men who are willing to undergo a vasectomy.[11]

> I always knew I didn't want to have children. When I was a little girl, everyone told me 'you're going through a phase, all little girls talk like you', but my opinions never changed. As I grew older, I became increasingly concerned about numbers of people, high-density living, poverty and other effects of over-population. Every day the news would carry stories about public services buckling under the strain of too many people and not enough money. By my twenties I knew I wanted a sterilisation and visited my GP. It was the beginning of a long uphill battle that I fought for several years. At first I would explain my reasons sensibly: 'I'm concerned about overpopulation, my intellectual and creative pursuits are too engrossing to want children and I'd like to be free of the hassle of contraceptives.' Various doctors placidly

ignored me and one referred me to a psychiatrist — the mere fact I'd made such an outlandish suggestion seemed to imply I was dysfunctional. Why is it so much harder to not have a baby than to have one — however bad a candidate for parenthood you might be? My father fought against fascism in the Italian Resistance and always told me that something is not necessarily true just because a majority of people uphold it as such. Had I claimed I was a violent criminal with anti-social tendencies, I expect I'd have got my sterilisation faster. Instead my whole family history was dragged up before a panel of medical experts before a date for the operation was eventually agreed. 4 April 1985, aged 28, unmarried, with no children, I eventually became truly myself. I have never had any doubts that what I did was right for me.

Elisa Roselli, 48, Italian, living in France

The negative aspects of population growth are two-fold:

Technically speaking, the first is 'visible' *over-crowding*. As the most densely populated country in Europe the UK is a good example of this, but it won't seem relevant to those who live in Canada or Scandinavia where there are plenty of wide, open spaces.

The second is less overt but more far-reaching and already affects everyone in the West regardless of our geographical location. This is *over-population*. Those of us who live in Europe, North America, parts of East Asia and Australasia may not have as many children as people in Africa or India, but we consume far greater quantities of the world's resources.

Rich nations take from poor nations by rapidly depleting the world's stock and by protecting their own interests.

Over-crowding and over-population are different, but often go hand in hand.

Over-crowding

Over-crowding is when too many people inhabit an area that isn't big enough for all of them to have a decent home, make a living and feel comfortable with their personal space. It can be measured differently in different countries, because some nationalities are better adapted to living close together. On buses and trains in the UK we place bags and coats on the empty seat next to us on the pretext of convenience but as much because we hope the seat will stay free. On Indian trains a local passenger will often sit next to you even if the rest of the carriage is empty, because personal space is a little known concept to him or her.

Japan has far more people per square mile than Canada, but Canada was settled by farmers and people are used to having space around them. Japanese people have lived in multi-family dwellings in cities for centuries because much of their land isn't arable. The country's birth rate is low, suggesting that people do take responsibility for their immediate environment. Japan's economic structure supports its population well and there is generally work and enough money for people to afford food and a home. Nobody feels hemmed in – road rage, for example, is unheard of.

Over-crowding creates social unrest when people feel threatened by the close proximity of others or when the system fails to support everyone and resources (housing and services) are divided unequally. If there's only one fire for 50 people to crowd around, those on the fringes will be left in the cold.

One crisp winter's day, friends and I joined a queue on the concrete paths that surround the ponds on Hampstead Heath. The queue consisted of families with young children, all of who stuck to the path. Soon we realised that they weren't queuing *for* anything, there were just so many people nobody could walk any faster. Gridlock! We might as well have been filing through post 9/11 airport immigration in the US. Maybe the council will build more tarmac paths across the fields (though then they won't be fields anymore) but, environmental consequences aside, where was the quality of life in that day for those families who'd fancied a stroll in the fresh air? Unhampered by the disagreeable combination of buggy wheels and long grass we left the path and climbed the hill.

Western governments react to population growth by providing more homes, roads, schools, paths and other facilities. Billions of pounds are poured into public services each year, but the electorate continues to complain that they need more. Nobody ever suggests that the reason services are over-burdened is that there are *too many people* trying to use them. I had a ring around Whitehall – home of the UK's central Government departments – about it but, as expected, it was impossible to get anyone to chat even informally on the subject.

The Department for the Environment, Food and Rural Affairs (DEFRA) said that while the *impact* of humans on the environment is their concern, the humans themselves are not their responsibility. DEFRA referred me to the Department of Health. The Department of Health said call Number 10. Number 10 suggested the Home Office, but the

right that treatment should be equally available to everyone who'd like a baby, but in the same way that some childfree people feel like second-class citizens in the workplace, many would rather that precious medical funding was spent on services everyone could benefit from.

It's worth noting that there are more than 5,000 children languishing on the adoption register in England and Wales alone. In the US the figure is 130,000. Some estimates say 44 million children in Africa, Asia, Latin America and the Caribbean will be orphaned by 2010 as a result of AIDS, poverty and war.[14]

> **So how many Planet Earths do you think we will need by 2050 to keep humankind in the style to which we have become accustomed? Two? Three? Half a dozen? It's an absurd question of course and there's an absurd answer as well: it's two. But it's nothing like as absurd as the fact that there's not a single world leader prepared to give more than the most spurious consideration to our imminent collision with ecological reality.**[15]
>
> ***Jonathan Porritt, chairman of the UK's Sustainable Development Corporation and former director of Friends of the Earth***

Over-population

Over-population is when resources are used more quickly than they can be replenished and when waste piles up more quickly than it can be disposed of. This doesn't only happen in poor countries. In the 1970s Florida's underground fresh water supply ran out and coastal areas became polluted because the sea couldn't dilute or carry away the waste that was dumped in it fast enough.[16]

Hong Kong has suffered from over-populated and over-crowded conditions for so long that until recently it was common to build hanging porches on the outside of multi-storey apartments in an attempt to gain a few feet of extra living space. The practice was banned after a series of catastrophes in which the hanging rooms fell and killed not only their occupants but some unfortunate pedestrians. Hong Kong's problems were countered to a degree when the harbour was filled with new buildings, but the knock-on effect was dead fish and no jobs for those traditionally employed as fishermen. Hong Kong's birth rate is very low.

Some countries are good at recycling the type of waste produced by our throwaway culture. Switzerland, Scandinavia and Canada all have effective means of safely breaking-down not only glass and paper, but plastics, packaging and batteries. But though the average person in the UK produces half a tonne of household rubbish each year, less than 12 per cent of the total gets recycled. Eight million nappies are chucked in the bin every day in Britain, along with all sorts of rubbish that contains chemicals and toxins. They don't decompose, they get buried in landfill sites.[17]

America has a worse record than Europe both for consumption and recycling. The average American gets through twice the annual amount of the average German,[18] and it's easy to see why. In Washington you stand in line for a breakfast pain au chocolat at 8 o'clock in the morning and get asked, 'Is that with syrup or ice-cream?' before being handed a polystyrene carton on a cardboard tray with a plastic knife and fork, all of which you throw away within minutes. In Berlin you get a plate.

Most of us are shielded from the damaging effects of over-population as we go about our comfortable lives, so it's easy to turn a blind eye and joke that environmentalists will have us knitting our own muesli before long. But population increase is such that the problems we're becoming aware of now will be a vivid and close reality for future generations.

Parents are often the ones to use saccharine phrases like 'we must protect the environment for our children and our children's children,' but they ignore the stark reality that reproduction itself is the single factor most likely to result in their descendants living in a hell hole. Given that selfishness is a term inextricably bound up in the childfree debate, it's odd that those who don't want children often feel more responsible for the world we'll leave behind us than those who do.

There are 6 billion people in the world
There will be five more when you finish reading this sentence
3,500 babies are born every 20 minutes
The population is growing by over 76 million people per year (the approximate population of Germany)
Meanwhile swathes of rainforest are cut down every second
More than one plant or animal species is lost every 20 minutes
Water tables are falling, coral reefs are dying, the ozone layer is thinning and oceans are being over fished

In the 30 years between 1970 and 2000, the number of vehicles on the world's roads grew from 246 million to 730 million and air traffic multiplied six-fold.

World Population Awareness

In Mexico City a recent scheme to cut down on terrible pollution and traffic jams backfired spectacularly. Cars with certain digits on their number-plate were permitted access to the city centre on Mondays, Wednesdays and Fridays only. Other digits were allowed in on Tuesdays and Thursdays, and drivers who used their cars on the wrong day were fined. Many drivers solved the inconvenience by purchasing a second car with the alternative plates.

> Children are generally concerned about environmental issues, but most adults live with severe disregard for nature and don't seem interested in changing.
>
> *Paulo, 30, teacher, Barcelona*

Anthropological evidence suggests that thousands of years ago population control was very much a part of life. Certain potions and herbs were thought to have contraceptive powers and one culture believed tying a rope around a woman's waist would prevent her getting pregnant. Remote cultures are often referred to as primitive but though their methods of sustaining their populations to ensure everyone got fed may have been so, they were way ahead of the inhabitants of today's sophisticated world in their environmental husbandry.

From CE 01 until a thousand years later, world population remained fairly static at around 300 million. It's only in the last 500 years (a tiny speck on the end of humankind's 50,000 years in existence) that living conditions and prospects for everyone improved enough for families to grow bigger. Once farmers learned the benefits of crop rotation and soil fertilisation, harvests became more bountiful and with good food in their tummies more children survived into adulthood. In the West the Industrial Revolution speeded things along. Cities began treating sewage and providing clean drinking water. People didn't start breeding like rabbits, they just stopped dying like flies.

World population subsequently grew steadily for a few hundred years, albeit with a small counter trend emerging in Europe towards the end of the 18th century. Here, the beginnings of huge social change were afoot and children were no longer regarded primarily as earners. Education became more widely available and, though parents wouldn't have been debating whether to send the kids to private school or the local comprehensive, they may have been considering if sending them to school at all might be better than ramming them up chimneys. Fewer children meant fewer mouths to feed and the prospect of a better life for the whole family.

A trip Jim and I took to India coincided with a family planning drive in one of the southern states. Huge billboards at the side of the main roads showed pictures of two different families side by side. On the left a smartly dressed, affluent looking mum and dad were cradling a plump baby. On the right was an image of abject poverty. A thin woman supping water from a dripping standpipe was surrounded by dozens of children, barefoot and clad in rags. To us the message was clear – having fewer babies could lift you out of the poverty trap. We had to wait a few hours for a bus, and sat on some rocks underneath one of the posters. Locals from the village brought us chai in clay cups and the poster proved a good topic of conversation. They were proud of its colourful presence in their rather dusty community although, it transpired, not for intended reasons. Maybe it was unfortunate that the affluent couple in the picture weren't smiling, but our new friends all felt the same. 'Very sad for the couple with only one baby,' they lamented. 'The second picture is like us – everyone is happy because God has blessed them with many children.'

Fertility rates in the world's poorer countries remain high. Apart from lack of alternative opportunities, social and religious pressures, the machismo idea of a man's virility being judged by the number of children he has is still evident. In affluent countries, women tend to be questioned more about not having children than men, but in poorer countries it's often the other way around. Jim and I were once interviewed about not having children as we gasped for air deep within the pitch-black bowels of a remote Bolivian silver mine. We'd ventured in to learn about the appalling conditions the miners work in, and what we saw was truly shocking.

The miners dig by hand and the heat, dust and claustrophobia are terrifying. Due to the high altitude they chew on coca leaves and sip a drink of 96 per cent alcohol to keep going. They die young of silicosis or liver rot and there are numerous accidents caused by explosives and rock falls. Our guide told us soberly that the miners have no choice but to do this work because most have seven or eight children to feed. When he asked us 'where our children were' he was visibly dumbfounded to hear that we didn't have any. 'Men from Gringolandia must be very lazy in the night!' he joked. (Gringolandia being the Bolivian vernacular for Europe.)

The story changes however, when traditionally large families from developing countries emigrate. In California, home to America's largest Hispanic population, state demographers recently scaled back their population projections for 2040 by nearly 7 million people, citing as a major reason the steady drop in the traditionally high fertility rate of Latina women.[19] Rocío Yñiguez, 35, who grew up in a family of nine in Jalisco, Mexico says she can't imagine having more than two children of her own because she doesn't want to diverge from the goal of work and a better quality of life that brought her to America in the first place. Family planners often use the phrase that aspiration is the best form of contraception. But older immigrant couples tend to stick to tradition and warn their children against having smaller families. Viviana Ablo de Moran is one of eleven children, none of whom were educated past elementary school. She worked in the fields in Mexico before meeting her husband and moving to the US, where she had five daughters, attempting to produce a boy to please her husband. 'I like the idea of a full dinner table at Thanksgiving and Christmas,' she says. 'I urge my daughters to think how they will feel with a table with just two children.'

The International Conference on Population takes place every four years. The United Nations invariably uses the opportunity to chastise western governments for not giving enough money to international family planning schemes – ideally more effective ones than the one we saw in India. When the conference was held in Mexico City in 1984, delegates were surrounded by the consequences of unchecked population growth. Only the wealthy can afford land and lots of people live in shacks. Food is relatively scarce, there are few economic opportunities, pollution, crime rates and disease are high, and hordes of unwanted children forage for scraps on the town's rubbish tips. In spite of this the US delegation to the conference, presumably staying in a smart hotel, announced it was severing funding for any family planning schemes that worked out of clinics where abortions were available. It happened during Ronald Reagan's presidency and was repealed by President Clinton in 1993, and re-instated by President Bush in 2001.[20]

In 1994 the conference was held in Cairo, and marked a turning point in attitudes towards birth control in the less developed world. For the first time, attending experts established a definite link between high fertility and the low status and self-esteem of women. Family planning advice issued to clinics in poor countries has subsequently focused on empowering women away from a life of perpetual reproduction.

In an article entitled 'Women and Self-Esteem',[21] American author Cara Swann reports that when women in any country are given the chance to have careers they gain a sense of self-worth through making a contribution to society in their own right. As a result, they have fewer children. In Brazil, TV soaps that have the nation hooked are packed with characters who work in business, as models and creative artists. Who knows what the plots are, but the programmes are being held responsible for moderating population growth, despite the heavy impact of Catholic opposition.

In an interview that she gave after adopting her small son from an orphanage in Cambodia (where she filmed the first *Tomb Raider* movie), the actress Angelina Jolie was asked if the experience made her want to have her own child. I read the article in print so her reaction wasn't visible, but I can't help thinking she must have considered it a somewhat bizarre question. Her reply was, 'No, not at all. Thinking of where Maddox might be now if I hadn't adopted him makes me want to adopt more children.'

In celebrity circles Nicole Kidman adopted two children when she and Tom Cruise were together and Jamie Lee Curtis, Calista Flockhart, Michelle Pfeiffer, Diane Keaton and Lynda La Plante also adopted their children. The numbers of single women who adopt is on the increase in the UK too. Many are professional, independent, unwilling to compromise with a partner who's not what they want and not keen on the assisted fertility route.

In Maori culture there's a saying, *Mai I te kopu kit e kohunga*, which translates roughly as 'from conception to grave, the child grows in the image of its parents'. Maoris believe nurture is stronger than hereditary ties, and happily bring up children who are not biologically their own.

Elsewhere, the majority of would-be parents are less compassionate. 'You don't know what you're getting' and 'adopted children have all sorts of problems' are common excuses for not considering the option, though plenty of mums and dads are surprised by their own children's personalities. You don't know what you're getting even if you give birth to it, in reality.

> I always longed for a family – a little boy and a little girl to keep each other company. After years of trying and not falling pregnant, we started IVF. I was in my thirties and felt time was running out, though we couldn't have afforded treatment before then anyway. Having a baby was all I ever thought about. Nothing else mattered to me, my every waking hour was spent yearning, hoping, wishing for a miracle. And it had to be a baby that came from my body, I felt that deeply and instinctively. I can't begin to describe how gruelling IVF was – the ups, the downs, the endless hospitals and doctors. It completely dominated our lives for years and tested our marriage to the limits. Sometimes I'd be so hopeful it had worked I'd go out and buy the odd item of baby clothing and hide it away at the bottom of a drawer. We had four IVF cycles and I did get pregnant, twice. Rob planted a rose in the garden the first time to celebrate. But a couple of weeks later, I lost the baby and five months later the same happened again. I wanted to die – to be with my babies who I'd wanted so badly for so many years. I was desperate, devastated, out of control with grief. Those years were so awful. I would never recommend IVF to anyone. My one regret is that Rob and I ever began it. Once you start it sucks you in and you can't stop thinking 'one

> more time, we'll just try one more time'. I am not the same woman I was before that treatment – it shattered my confidence. We stopped having IVF in 1998, and by 2001 we'd adopted baby James. We were parents at last, after 19 years of trying! Looking back I can't believe we didn't consider adoption earlier, but it is a big decision and it must be right for you. You have to be strong and prepared for the scrutiny of the social services assessment. Adoption is a wonderful thing and I realise now that people who have a natural child don't know how things will turn out either. I'd never thought about the growing population I must admit – but it does make sense to adopt doesn't it? We are doing our bit and I feel good about that. James has helped to restore my belief in myself. He has made us so happy. Hand on heart I can honestly say we would not feel any different about him if he had been born to us. He is our baby! We would lay down our lives for him.
>
> *Anne, 40, Wales*

In 2004, the German Chancellor Gerhard Schroder and his wife adopted a three-year-old girl from a Russian orphanage. In keeping with the rest of Europe, Germany's birth rate is low. The Chancellor gave an interview in which he described his new daughter Victoria as a 'wonderful child' and encouraged German people with a place in their hearts and their homes to think if they too might like to adopt. 'There are many children,' he concluded, 'who can be offered a better future than the one they have.'[22]

Claire Rayner
agony aunt
b 1931

If women choose not to have children of course that's fine. It's a perfectly reasonable decision. Plenty of women have marvellous lives without children – my daughter is one of them. My two boys have young families and I have three grandsons. We all get along terribly well but I am very lucky.

I always say I lived the 1960s at belly level. I was either pregnant or patting a small child on the head. But plenty of women I knew then loved the freedom the pill allowed and had a wonderful sexy time and never had children. There was that horrid word 'barren' at that time and I'm very glad that's gone. Attitudes have changed. Having children was more of a status thing then. I'm not sure that exists today except maybe in the conurbations, where if you are the only girl on your estate who's not pregnant at 20, you feel a failure.

I'm surprised to hear there is still a stigma about women who choose not to have children. I would have thought it was the other way and people would be quicker to disapprove of large families, because we are so much more aware of the environment now. It's sad that women who want babies are increasingly unable to have them, but maybe that is nature trying to tell us that the world is overcrowded. There are more fertility problems than in the past and women often leave it too late so the birth rate is falling of its own accord really. Apparently, if you put rats in a cage with plenty of room they mate like billy-o until the cage gets crowded, then the younger ones don't reproduce. I think the same is happening with people.

Chapter 7
Work and Childcare

Man may toil from sun to sun,
But woman's work is never done.
Ancient couplet

While men have fathered children and maintained their careers with minimal inconvenience since time immemorial, modern women with a career and young family are not only left to shoulder the childcare, but subjected to greed-laden criticisms of the 'wanting-it-all' variety. As one friend says, 'The stereotype of the working mother is true. The mobile is clamped between my ear and my shoulder and my hands are plastered in glitter and glue. I'm trying to sound to my boss that our company share price is what I care about most in the world. He doesn't know, and he certainly doesn't care, that Phoebe is clinging onto my legs as I cram chocolate biscuits into her mouth in a desperate bribe for silence.'

In 1950's America, Adlai Stevenson* proclaimed to gathered students at a graduation speech:

> **Women's education is just the right preparation for their important future roles as the wives and mothers of the men who will make a difference in this world.**

It might seem outdated but not much has changed, because when women entered the workforce, nobody took up the role of Wife for them.

Men in general face less judgement than women. In office situations a man can proudly announce that he's leaving to pick up his children from school in the middle of the day while a mother, stretched to the limit, sits worrying at her desk rather than ask to attend an emergency because she will be viewed as neurotic and disorganised. (Women have played a part in this with still prevalent Mrs Bennet-like behaviour. On the rare occasions when Man Leaving Early struts from the office to go get his kids, we still have a tendency to simper admiringly as though he's just clinched world peace.)

In 2002, an extensive Women and Work Survey[1] found that more than three-quarters of the 5,000 women questioned felt that overworking was damaging their health. Nine out of ten were worn out by their stressful lifestyles. Half spent lunch-breaks dealing with child-related issues and the same number found fitting exercise into their lives

* Democrat Adlai Stevenson lost to Richard Nixon in the 1952 Presidential election. College graduates who listened to his speech that day included Sylvia Plath.

impossible. More than 80 per cent said it is they rather than their partners who have to take time off work to care for their children when they're ill.

Wealthy couples who can afford an army of nannies may escape years of tense, nervous headaches, but for vast numbers of working women, childcare structures and parental role-sharing are not sufficiently developed to make a balanced life feasible. Add to the juggler's props a spinning top of guilt. Time at work is spent worrying about the children and regretting missing out on their growing-up years.

Rachel and David both have demanding jobs. Rachel in law, David in the construction industry. Rachel is paid for four days but never works less than a 40-hour week. David works full time and is paid accordingly. They have two children, Zoe, 4, and Elliot, 2:

> The alarm rings at 6.20. There's no such thing as calm in our house, it's mad until we get the children out of the door at ten to eight. This can take longer than you'd imagine. Life is a permanent process of negotiation in which the adult doesn't seem to hold many cards. Zoe has strong opinions about what she wants to wear and though I begin by saying no to some of her suggestions, it's not unusual to be strapping her into the car seat in a flamboyant fairy outfit that's only meant for dressing up. Sometimes we leave the house several times before we get away. I often find myself scampering around upstairs with one eye on the clock, searching for a particular toy or nail

varnish that one of them insists they can't go to nursery without. I don't enjoy the morning run because I don't like saying goodbye. Sometimes they don't want to go in and it's a strong emotional pull. My drive to work takes an hour. I have to pay the congestion charge because we live in London and the nursery is one side of the zone and my office is on the other. David and I organise our lives via hands-free mobile phone in the car, which is about the only time I get to myself. It's not a relaxing start to the day.

I have breakfast at my desk and my job is non-stop stressful. Mothers who say they go into work for a rest must have very easy jobs or very difficult children! I grab a sandwich at lunchtime. 15 minutes away from my desk. I'm well paid, but at £70 per day per child, most of my salary goes to the nursery.

I need to leave work at five to collect Zoe and Elliot but I rarely manage it, which makes the drive across town very tense if I hit traffic. I never get all my work done. I leave emails unread and I'm always talking on my mobile as I drive, worrying if I'll have to pay the £1 per minute overtime fee that the nursery charges. The children and I usually get home around 6.30, and through the front door about 6.45; Elliot's going through a phase where he wants to do everything for us, including getting the key in the lock. I make their tea and they watch some TV. My children know quite a lot about TV. David gets home around eight so I usually do baths. Often Elliot wees in the water as soon as I put him in and we have to begin all over again.

The demands go on all evening. David's idea of childcare differs to mine. He'll sit the children in front of the telly and use the computer until they shout for something, but I want to spend time with them because I haven't seen them all day. We started giving Zoe some time on the computer and now Elliot wants his turn too so bedtime is getting later. It can take ages to get them to lie down by the time we've read stories and said good night to all the toys. After David and I have eaten (I'm an expert at making healthy suppers in half an hour), I usually have to do a couple of hours work. I managed, after a struggle, to negotiate a four-day working week. It means I have Fridays at home, but I still have to make up the work. I've been trying to have an early night for months. I like to read in bed, it's my relaxing time, so our light goes out around midnight. I don't sleep well, I wake up worrying. David and I just about hold things together but there's no slack. If something unexpected happens everything falls apart. We pick ourselves up again but it's exhausting sometimes. I never catch up with everything that needs to be done in our lives. I can completely understand why people wouldn't want to live like this. As for me it's mad I know, but I'd love another baby!

A lot of women get restless in their thirties and say that having children seemed like a time for new beginnings – a mid-life Phase Two. While some embrace the all-consuming nature of new motherhood, others find the same contentment wallowing in the luxury of time. Even if you lead a frenetic childfree life, there's at least opportunity to eat well and exercise, sleep well and socialise.

The theory that *less is more* is in the ascendant. There's even a growing international movement called 'In Praise of Slow',[2] which challenges the western message that faster equals better. It focuses on a lifestyle revolution in which quality overcomes our obsession with quantity, enabling us to lead more productive and fulfilling lives.

> **How sorry she felt for white people, who were always dashing around and worrying themselves over things that were going to happen anyway. What use was it having all that money if you could never sit still or just watch your cattle eating grass?**
>
> **None, in her view, none at all, and yet they did not know it. Every so often you met a white person who understood, who realised how things really were; but these people were few and far between and the other white people often treated them with suspicion.**
>
> *Precious Ramotswe, Botswana, from* The No. 1 Ladies' Detective Agency *by Alexander McCall Smith*

The last census of the UK's adult population[3] showed that in couples where both partners are employed, men spend half the time on childcare as women, even when their working hours are equal. In the US, women spend 22 hours per week on 'household activities' while men average ten. One in five men is 'involved' (which could presumably mean anything upwards of a pat on the head) in the care of pre-school children.[4]

Scandinavia has a large number of so-called househusbands and is generally considered a world leader in family provision. In Denmark, 70 per cent of day care centres are municipal and the Danish Government funds up to eight hours of childcare per day.[5] Is it purely coincidence that their kids speak fluent English and snack on crudités?

In the UK, local authorities can fund 12 hours of childcare per week.[6] As part of the Childcare Revolution,[7] there are plans to keep primary schools open between 8 am and 6 pm to allow parents a full day's work, but even those responsible for the policy slip into gender inequality in their briefings. When I enquired for more details a male civil servant told me with great enthusiasm, 'We're saying this plan must pass the *Guildford Test*, where a mum can drop off her child for all-day affordable childcare before travelling to London for a full day's work.'

Dad presumably will be getting up in his own time and enjoying a leisurely breakfast before buying a paper and pottering down to the station.

After a baby, most women downshift to work that is lower paid, of lower status and fails to use their skills. Women working part-time earn on average 40 per cent less per hour than men working full-time. There's a shortage of high quality part-time jobs and discrimination and lesser opportunities for women are reportedly 'deeply ingrained' in British culture.[8]

Trish, 35 from Tewkesbury, Gloucestershire works three days a week as a manager in a department store and cares for her daughter Alice, 2, on the remaining days.

The pluses are:

1. You get that Friday feeling on a Wednesday!
2. My work-life balance tips in favour of life.
3. I get the benefit of adult conversation three days a week. Four days of toddler interrogation is charming and funny, but full-time could feel like torture.
4. I have a varied week so I don't get bored.
5. Three days a week I eat a civilised lunch and wear nice clothes.

The minuses are:

1. I don't feel like a real member of my work team anymore.
2. My part-time status is not respected. I often have to take work calls while I'm chasing Alice around a playgroup.
3. I feel guilty and threatened in my job if I take time off when Alice is sick.
4. There is always a niggling thought at the back of my mind that a child should be cared for by its mother.
5. I have two deserving masters and I feel like I work a ten-day week.

We may be beginning to see the emergence of a pattern that can only cause a deeper divide between mothers and childfree women. It's becoming ever more apparent that combining work and childcare is not an option that allows balance in a woman's life. But while increasing numbers react by ditching motherhood, a counter development has emerged even within the last three years. The newest research comparable to the Women and Work survey 2002 (page 106), suggests more women are reverting to a traditional stereotype to combat the problem. In results that would frustrate some of our grandmothers, most questioned said they're no longer bothered about keeping a good job after having a baby and two-thirds agreed that 'a man should be the main provider for his family'.[9]

Currently, perceived injustice at work is the most overt example of the polarisation of parents and non-parents – modern offices are run on a system of divide and drool. A new vocabulary has even evolved: Childfree employees are DINKS (Double Income No Kids) or THINKERS (Two Healthy Incomes No Kids Early Retirement). Parents suffer such labels as 'fertile freeloaders' and 'tele-shirkers' – the inference being that they pretend to be working away from the office when they're really having a day out with the kids.

Governments have pushed so-called family-friendly policies to the top of their political agendas. They need to capture parental votes, but the policy reaches into the heart of public life and affects all of us, regardless of whether or not we have children. Decisions on childcare provision and its funding will have long-term consequences not only for children themselves, but for the economy, the role of women in the workforce and the concurrent drive to eradicate poverty, which is based on the theory that the childcare needs of poorer parents must be met to enable them to go out to work and bring home a salary.

For employers too, family-friendly is the corporate watchword of the new century, but it's brought forth a modern malaise. Offices, factories, surgeries, shops and studios are having to cope with increasing incidents of Job Jealousy – between those who want time for their children and those who want time for other pursuits.

Plenty of employers need convincing that such policies are fair for them. Some claim that flexible working is bad for business and actively want to discriminate against parents because of their 'inconvenient' need for flexibility. One director of a recruitment agency tells of being approached by a businessman client enquiring how to devise a method of skewing recruitment in favour of young, single people. The client favoured tapping into the gay workforce to limit the money he had to pay out through maternity and paternity leave. 'Plenty of employers want to keep families out,' the director admitted.

It also seems inevitable, if illegal, that there are sectors where women will be discriminated against because some employers hire a male candidate who 'won't be off to have a baby'.

Childcare is a magical password. Whispering it in the context of leaving work early or arriving late protects employees from disapproving remarks about inconvenience and lack of commitment to their jobs. But everyone is fed up with working long hours – parents and non-parents alike. Surveys consistently show that most workers would opt for time-off over a pay rise.

> If I took the afternoon off because the dog had a cold, my colleagues wouldn't accept it for one moment. But if I had a child, they'd be falling over themselves to let me go home. Why should parents get more

> breaks? Flexible holidays, time off for school plays, paternity leave. I don't resent them having it but what am I getting? And I do the same day's work.
>
> *Ed, Gloucestershire*

The term Family Friendly tends to exclude adult relatives. It's grown out of the assumption that people still live in convenient units of adults *and* children, even though that's not the case any more. When a politician gets sacked for example, the common euphemism is 'he'll be spending more time with his family.' And sure enough, he's always appeared in the following day's papers, photographed with his wife, children and usually a Labrador to complete the stereotype. But times are changing (even within the walls of traditional institutions like the Palace of Westminster). We've all heard the phrase 'friends are the new family' and childfree people often consider themselves to be 'families of two'. Our use of language is outdated and the word 'family' needs to be expanded to include more mixed relationship arrangements. It might be possible nowadays for the hapless MP to appear in the press with a same sex partner or alongside his Mum and Dad, but it's unlikely the caption would read 'pictured with his family' unless there were children. If it ever does, we'll know we've modernised.

> I hate when people say 'Does your sister have a family?' Doh! The clue is in the question.
>
> *Lottie, 50, insurance clerk, Florida*

It's not uncommon for childfree people to hear remarks such as, 'Oh, so you don't have a *real* family then?' or 'Oh, so you don't have a family *of your own*?' At best this is patronising and at worst insulting - because of course we consider our siblings, parents and the rest of the motley crew to be our families: Our *own*, *real* families!

It may seem a pedantic point but if the word family is *not* attributed to all members, adult dependents will lose out and children alone will be considered worthy beneficiaries of policies that help working people to juggle their lives.

Family Friendly is misleading. The policies we are seeing introduced are, more accurately, *Child* Friendly.

Even if childfree people don't have dependent relatives, they do have engagements in their lives that they consider valuable. The majority of employers and colleagues, who tend to have children however, deem them less important. Some even brand their childfree colleagues ungenerous if they refuse to alter their own lives to accommodate a parental duty.

> I eavesdropped on a conversation at work once after I refused to step in for a colleague who wanted an afternoon off for a school swimming gala. She and another woman were bitching about me — saying I'd said no to spite her because I didn't have a boyfriend or children of my own. What struck me as stupid is that the woman she was complaining to refused to cover as well. But she had children so it's like they were on the same side.
>
> *Miranda, 39, IT consultant, Auckland, New Zealand*

Childfree people (or those assumed to have 'fewer ties') aren't bound by term-time, but as anyone who's tried to organise a holiday with a group of friends or a working partner knows, co-ordinating arrangements is always difficult.

> I felt I was being blamed for being single when I asked if I could take holiday over Easter. I wanted to go walking in the Lake District with my brothers but my boss turned down my request. He said I was young and free and could go away at any time. But one of my brothers is in the Army and was only home for a week. The parents in my office took all of Easter off and so did my boss. But he didn't seem to think my time restraints had any significance.
>
> *Adam, 25, mechanic*

Sometimes employers just go for the easiest option if they're short-staffed. Why ask the woman with children to stay late when you know she has childcare issues? But the childfree person feels obliged to help out. It would take a brave person to tell the boss, 'I have to leave at five, I'm cooking my mum's tea.'

> In a newsroom the size of ours there are never enough people on hand to cover for the unexpected. Journalists are routinely called upon to work overtime at short notice. I don't mind working Lates or Earlies, it's an accepted part of life in the industry, but seeing your name on the rota alongside some regular day duties guarantees a smile. Last Friday, a call came into the office at 5.30, just as I was about to go home. There'd been a chemical spill from a lorry. I'd timed my day to perfection because, for the first time

> in months, I was free to take a young lady I'd met for dinner. When that call came in my evening went down the drain. Rhiannon who I'd been working with has a baby and I knew there'd be no question who stayed behind. I cancelled my date and spent the evening tracking down witnesses, interviewing police officers and hanging around the local hospital in the freezing cold. By the time I'd filed my copy and got home it was half-past ten. I do like my job and I do feel parents should be supported in the workplace, but it doesn't seem right that it's in preference to non-parents, does it? It's the Christmas party soon, and I know what that will be like. My colleagues with kids will be handing round photos of their cherub-cheeked angels for all of us to coo over, and I won't even have a girlfriend to take along.
>
> *John, 40, regional newspaper reporter, Wales*

Some childfree people have big chips on their shoulders and their bleating that 'it's not fair!' is redolent of the children they're moaning about. To others, a few extra hours in the office is a small price to pay for the freedoms bestowed by not being permanently bound to a school timetable. Most aren't whingeing, they just want their own lives to be respected in the way that parents' lives automatically are.

> In the job I'm in now there are women who routinely fill in sick leave forms when they take time off to care for their children. I feel this is unfair because the parent herself isn't ill. Sometimes the child isn't

> ill either, but maybe the nanny is or the teacher is. If I need a day off – say there's water pouring through my ceiling or my car needs emergency treatment – I wouldn't dream of pretending I was ill. When I returned to the office I'd fill in an annual leave form. I worked nightshifts for a spell years ago and all my colleagues were single like me. There was a team of staff on duty during the day too and most of them had children. I can see it would be hard for them to be heading into work just as school finished, but I did feel fed up at getting all the night shifts. Maybe it is easier for single people to work overnight, but it doesn't mean they want to or should have to anymore than anyone else. It felt like if we didn't have children our lives were less important.
>
> *Sue, 50, service industry telephonist, Glasgow*

In a statutory sense there's limited provision for non-parents to take time away from work at short notice. It varies from country to country and managers can exercise discretion. But grey legislation tends to be interpreted to the effect that a mother can take her child to the doctor's surgery on a weekday morning, but a childless person is expected at her desk at 9 am sharp, even if her house burned down in the night.[10]

Parents often complain that they're sidelined at work, but compromise is usually accepted as a necessary component of life, so it makes sense that those who've decided against having children can get ahead faster at work if they're ambitious. Amateur athletes are dedicated to their sport but, though training commitments aren't compatible with a rise up the greasy pole to a smart MD's office, you don't hear them moan about lack of career status (or failing social life).

> **For all they go on about how rewarding their children are, too many working parents still seem to think that no price should be paid for being blessed with them. They don't only want to knock off at 5 pm sharp – they want to make sure no-one else is staying late at the office earning extra brownie points once they've gone home. But childless people can afford to be more single minded about their careers. If they've put in more hours, why shouldn't they be rewarded? So many working parents want to see the playing field levelled down, not levelled up. It's a classic case of the politics of envy, the visceral hatred for those who have any advantage in life that you don't.**
>
> *Julian Baggini, broadsheet columnist and editor of* **The Philosophers' Magazine**

The true injustice is that sufficient and fair structures have not been established for anyone with commitments outside the workplace since women left their traditional supporting roles to earn money. It's still nearly always mothers who complain that they're sidelined at work. There's no ongoing debate about whether it's viable to combine fatherhood with a career.

In the UK, moves are afoot to try to level the playing field, but progress is slow. Expanding work-life balance policies beyond the improved childcare provision designed to help parents will take years. There'll never come a day when time off for an art class is accommodated as swiftly as time off for childcare, but it does seem unreasonable that while a mother is unquestioningly granted paid maternity leave perhaps two or three times in her career, a childfree person seeking an unpaid career break is invariably turned down. A projected 60 per cent of women and 40 per cent of men in the UK will take up maternity/paternity leave at least once in the course of their working lives. At the statutory benefit rate of £100 per week, it translates into £148 million per week spread across all tax-payers, regardless of whether they have children themselves.[11]

In the same way that many mothers give up work because of a lack of childcare support, high numbers – again usually women – are lost from the workforce each year in categories where personal circumstances were not chosen: for instance, people who have elderly dependents requiring care; people who suffer from chronic illness or disability; or people who have a temporary crisis such as bereavement.

Many people would love the opportunity to take time out of a profession to study but, although this would benefit employers, it isn't considered worthy of compensation.

We see advantages being given to people who choose to have children at the expense of everyone else. Having children is a lifestyle choice and is certainly not the only domestic reason for needing time off work. In the course of my work as a charity personnel director I see many people struggling with the day-to-day demands of their domestic lives. This can be because they're caring for an elderly or sick relative, they have a housing crisis or are dealing

with the impact of a recent bereavement. If governments believe family-friendly working policies improve productivity of people in the workplace, why are they not introducing an entitlement to emergency leave for everyone, rather than making a special case for those who choose to have children?

Sheila Cunliffe, Kidding Aside
(the UK's childfree network)

> I have never wanted children. As a child I assumed I would 'grow out of it' as I grew up but I never have, and I have to say the older I get, the more I don't want children. The childfree lifestyle is not embraced here in NZ, quite the opposite since we are constantly reminded of the dangers of the falling birth rate and the Government keeps coming up with new ways of rewarding people for having children. The best things about being childfree are freedom to do what you want, the ability to focus on your career, extra money to spend on yourself, and I have to admit – not having to be around children.
>
> *Melanie, 34, industrial electrician, Auckland, New Zealand*

The UK Government currently spends around £2.5 billion annually[12] on state childcare. The demand is huge and, in addition to the state, lottery money has funded a big increase in after-school clubs in recent years. Childfree people don't add to the burden on overstretched resources (schools, hospitals, etc), but they do put money into the pot. Tax contributions in theory enhance living conditions for us all, whether or not we directly benefit from the services they provide. Education is the key to a civilised society and the principles of the NHS are still revered around the world. But though like death, taxes are one of life's certainties, it doesn't mean we have to like them.

> I feel bitter about how my hard earned money is spent by the Government. Parents get a lot more support than non-parents. They all seem to have two cars, holidays and mobile phones, and yet I see my elderly dad struggling on his pension. None of it goes on the things I'd like. The roads near me are in a bad state. Taxpayers' money is never used to mend potholes, but hardly a week goes by without another traffic calming scheme being built outside a school.
>
> *Eileen, 45*

In *The Baby Boon: How Family-Friendly America Cheats the Childless*, author Elinor Burkett brands the childcare revolutions currently prioritised by Western governments as overtly discriminatory. 'Parents are getting more than non-parents,' she says, 'childless people are being relegated to second-class citizens.'

In America parents can claim approximately US$1,000 (£550/A$1,300 appx) annual tax credit for each of their children, and the Australian package offers yearly payments for each child and a lump sum of A$2,414 (£1,000/US$1,858) on the birth of every new baby. (The latter is an alternative to paid maternity leave, which is not compulsory in Australia.) When Mussolini was in power, he too made parenthood a political issue by awarding tax rebates for every child born along with the motto '5 million more Italians means 5 million more bayonets'. In Italy today, family credit increases per each child born.[13]

In the UK, the Chancellor recently introduced a £250 (US$450/A$600 appx) one-off voucher payment (the Child Trust Fund) for every baby born on or after 1 September 2002. The vouchers can be invested in a variety of ways, and only accessed by the child himself when he reaches eighteen. In addition parents can claim annual Child Tax Credit and Working Tax Credit, that differs in amount depending on circumstance. Those who employ nannies can claim between £7,000 and £10,000 (US$13000-8,500/A$17000-24000 appx) per year to offset the cost.[14] For many middle class families where both parents work nannies are indispensable and have their employers over a barrel, commanding high salaries, accommodation, cars and even tennis lessons.

Even though millions are paid out in such benefits, parents still feel under supported and the UK has one of the highest rates of child poverty in the developed world.[15] Around 0.5 per cent of the UK's GDP is spent on childcare at present, but campaigners for improvement would like to see it rise to between 2 per cent and 2.5 per cent. This is the figure in Denmark.[16]

Commercial futurists who predict coming trends expect life-work balance issues to dominate political debate for years to come. 'Eveolution' will become shorthand for the impact of women on business. 'Eternity Leave' will allow employees time off to care for sick friends or relatives.[17]

Shirley Conran
founder, The Work Life Balance Trust; author, *Superwoman*, 1978
b 1932

When I wrote *Superwoman* it was seized upon like a modern Bible. Women then were wanting to lead more interesting lives away from the kitchen, but even if we'd been out to work all day we were expected to put children to bed, slip into something glamorous and rustle up a three course meal for our husbands. I offered tips on how to do it all, but now I revoke that approach.

> ***Your husband will never regard your work as anything but tiresome. Be sensible enough to shut up when the caveman in him surfaces.***

Life is still too short to stuff a mushroom, but now I'd say if you're enjoying yourself without children, don't have them. Think for yourself and don't be influenced into having children because it's what everyone else is doing. Ask yourself 'what will life really be like as a mother?'

Women of my generation who tried to work and raise a family were pioneers.

But nothing has moved on. In the UK, it's just as impossible to have a decent quality of life now, if you try to combine both.

I still resolutely believe that mothers who go out to work are more fulfilled than those who don't.

> ***A working woman is not so likely to cling to her children when it's their turn to leave the nest. A working mother has her own interests, and children with working mothers don't suffer from 'smother-love.'***

The Work Life Balance Trust campaigns for improved support for working mothers.

I see a trend emerging among the women I visit in offices in the course of my work.

There's a real divide. The staff who have children spend their lunch hour frantically food-shopping on the internet and having hushed and anxious conversations with stressed-out husbands and babysitters. They're permanently exhausted and haven't had a new coat for ten years. The non-mothers are looking at the lives of their colleagues and making a decision it's not for them. They're popping out for a sandwich and a chat at lunchtime and talking about their plans for the evening or weekend. Why would anyone actively choose the first lifestyle?

As for working part-time, it seems to involve twice the work for half the money with none of the office perks or protection.

The majority of intelligent women are likely to find their careers are sidelined – theirs, not their husbands – and their independence is lost. There's rarely an extended family on hand to help with the kids and the public infrastructure is not in place instead. Arranging a career around school and finding an affordable nanny can be a nightmare. Parents are paying ridiculous prices for homes near a decent secondary school – never mind if it's where they'd like to live. You're well out of it.

I have my two boys and let's just say that I'm very glad I didn't have a third child. There was this thing, with Terence and me, wanting a girl. But I'm so glad I didn't and I would absolutely not have children now. You're signing yourself up for 24/7 guilt and anxiety and I wouldn't do it again. Everyone knows about the tantrums, the teenagers with loud stereos and inappropriate boyfriends or girlfriends, but nobody tells you how never-ending motherhood is and that's what

I struggle with. They are always your children, even when they're adults and adult problems of depression, debt and failed relationships are bigger and scarier than those of a toddler who wets his bed or steals sweets in the supermarket. The responsibility of parenthood is overwhelming and incredibly stressful. And it's for life.

Don't give up a pleasant life, for a life of unpaid drudgery. Your standard of living drastically declines, and the kids take off as soon as they can, without a backward glance.

Chapter 8
Men

When a woman announces she's pregnant,
50 per cent of men break open the champagne
and 50 per cent think their lives are over.
Paulo, Barcelona

Most male animals are pre-programmed to copulate and run. Time spent nurturing babies is time lost to their sole motivation of inseminating more females. They can't spare the time to hang around the den or the lair because they need to get out and chase more women. Female animals on the other hand have invested substantially more time nurturing the embryo (three months gestation for lions and tigers, 22 months for an elephant), and therefore have a far stronger instinct of care. As a result, they tend to stay home once their babies are born.

In the 17th century, Ismail the Bloodthirsty of Morocco fathered 900 children. He didn't do much of the childcare either.

> **[In history] children existed solely to inherit a man's genes, his moral code and his name. This was taken for granted among the aristocracy, but merchants, craftsmen and peasants also bought into the idea. That has all gone now and there is nothing for my son to inherit. I have no craft to teach him, I haven't a clue what he might do when he's older. By the time he grows up, the world will be completely different. That's how we live now. For a man to bring a child into the world is meaningless.**
>
> ***Michel Houellebecq, author of* Atomised**

The sexes appear to become defined at a very young age. When asked if she wants children when she grows up – Sophie, who's eight, can talk at length about how many she'll have and in what order; her favourite names are even picked out. But ask ten-year-old brother Tom the same question and he makes a gurning 'we've got a right one 'ere' face and says he's never thought about it. It's hard to determine if adult men are as interested in having children now that we're out of the Flintstone era as they were when species survival was imperative.

> My wife didn't want children, which made me think for myself. If I'd met someone different I'd just have assumed it was what you did. I feel I've had a lucky escape.
>
> *Neil, 42, Railtrack manager, London*

> I would love to have lots of children. My father was one of eighteen – there were two sets of triplets in his

> family – and my Mum is one of twelve. I have six brothers and sisters. Looking after my siblings hasn't put me off having kids of my own – quite the opposite.
>
> *Jason, 24, student, Wellington, New Zealand*

> The wife wanted kids and I went along with it, but I wasn't bothered either way.
>
> *Ken, 58, taxi driver*

In the way that some men seem detached from the prospect of fatherhood, some are perplexed by the miracle of birth. 'Do you like him then?' one mother resorted to asking when her boyfriend wondered about a pint before passing comment on his new son. Another gave his wife an hour to recover before unpacking carpet tile samples for her to flip through.

I went to interview the editor of the UK's bestselling men's magazine, in the hope of tapping into the male psyche:

> **Babies are banned from the magazine. I feel strongly that guys who read GQ don't want that. We do big emotional issues but we don't pepper the magazine with titbits about when is the right time to start a family. Even if you're a parent, which I am, you don't want to read about kids all the time. I couldn't love my kids more, I'm obsessed with them, but in a magazine I want to read about the car I can't afford or the great holiday I might be able to afford.**
>
> **We are men, we just don't have the same aspirations as women. We hang on longer when it comes to any sort of commitment. Most of us will try to put**

off big decisions like having children for as long as possible. We have to be dragged kicking and screaming to the altar because every man wants to be a bachelor for as long as possible. Women are getting married later too, but even if a woman wanted to settle down and start a family during her optimum baby-making years, she'd probably find it hard to meet a guy in his twenties willing to do so. In today's culture men don't have to make a sudden switch from being an adolescent to looking into that tunnel of drudgery – you can be a teenager into your fifties if you want. Men are dumb. Men aren't as sophisticated as women. They might have a vague idea about settling down and having a family sometime, but without coercion they'd reach 60 and suddenly go, 'Oh shit, I forgot to get married and have kids, how stupid of me.' It's never like, 'Hey I'm 18, I want a wife and a baby now.' Men are quite happy bouncing along from one relationship to another with no great plan to their lives. We're lucky we're pushed into getting married and having kids because they are the most gratifying things in our lives. If a woman is not a mother or not considering becoming a mother, she is sexually far more attractive to men. A mother can of course be a sexual being, but she's also a mother.

As editor of the magazine it's not my job to tell everyone else about the joys of being a father. It's fine to talk about the joys of buying a vintage Aston Martin – but I think it's a bit facile to do that.

ND: To talk about the joys of buying a vintage Aston Martin?
No. To talk about the joys of fatherhood.

Dylan Jones, editor, GQ

Headlines from men's magazines:

Ultimate Firepower – 6 billion pounds of stuff that goes boom!

FHM

What women want. And when. And where and, ooh! Yeah, right there!

GQ

Get into the groove. Sex tips for frustrated fathers.

Fathers Quarterly

I decided not to have children when I was in my late teens/early twenties. I then gave myself ten years to change my mind before having a vasectomy to ensure I was sterile. I found that I could justify having children only on the basis of purely selfish and hormonal reasons. I could not justify adding to human overpopulation, which is degrading the environment and our eco-system. I enjoy my freedom and independence and the disposable income I have available to me. I would not enjoy the noise and mess which is found in households with children and I am happy to avoid the more stressful aspects of parenting.

Reactions toward me are almost always negative, especially from those with children. I have now given up trying to explain my reasons for choosing to be childless because it often provokes a hostile or aggressive reaction. I believe people with children find these issues challenging and react with guilt when their own selfishness is implied.

1. They assume that other people are willing to tolerate noise/disturbance from their children (eg using supermarkets as playgrounds, bringing children into the office).
2. Parents appear unable or unwilling to understand or value people who have chosen to be childfree.
3. Women often complain about having children, even though contraception is now freely and widely available. (My ex-wife was once rounded on at a female-only coffee morning when she mentioned she did not have children: 'Just wait – your turn will come,' was the response.)
4. There is a lack of positive parenting which is contributing to anti-social behaviour in our society. Children grow up expecting instant gratification.
5. Women at work openly discuss pregnancy, childbirth and the messier aspects of parenting that I don't find appealing to listen to.

There is increasing discrimination in the workplace in favour of women (and men) with children. On a number of occasions I have been forced to do the work of pregnant colleagues, and those on maternity/ paternity leave, in addition to coping with my own workload. I am also beginning to resent having to work full office hours when pregnant women and those with children are given time off and allowed flexi hours.

Although I came under some emotional pressure from my mother, who wanted grandchildren, I believe that childfree women have a much rougher time than men because women are often 'expected' to have children by family and peers.

S, 55, salesman, Birmingham.

My early adulthood was spent in Sydney where I worked as an architect. Australia was the land of lotus-eaters then. We had such a great time I have no idea why anyone would think a child could have enhanced it. We'd get our coffee in the morning, go to work, and then it was down to the beach to swim or surf. There was time for quiet contemplation as the sun went down. We were free.

My girlfriend at the time got pregnant because of a failed IUD. It was and still is the worst news I have ever had in my life. I had to take a flight to Berlin for work and I sat on the plane feeling suicidal. Both of us knew we were having a fling, it was never meant to be a long-term relationship, but K always imagined she'd have kids one day and wouldn't have considered not going ahead with the birth. Of course I didn't pressure her, I'm not that low.

We drew up a practical plan. I would stick by her while the baby was small and be dad for two years until he was out of nappies and she was on top of things. I feel I accepted my responsibilities. I was there at J's birth, which was very moving. There were lovely moments in his babyhood. He'd crawl up to me and climb all over me while I was napping on the sofa. He was cute and lovable. But I never changed my mind. You might like working in a café but if you won the lottery you'd stop. K and I stuck to our plan. J is now in his early twenties and we're friends.

Years later when I was living in England I fell in love with a different woman – L. I knew from the start that she wanted a large family and she knew that I didn't. Maybe I should have moved on earlier but it takes two, and she was convinced that if we had a baby I'd love it so much I'd want more. For 12 years this was the undercurrent of our relationship. As L got older and felt time was running out we had to make a decision. I didn't want to lose her and she didn't want to leave me, so we compromised. I agreed to 'one baby and one only'. It's the price I paid to stay with her. I was in my late thirties when we got together and I didn't feel my chances of meeting someone as nice as L were that great.

We have a little boy who is six. He's gorgeous, I love him, but once again I would never have chosen

> to have him and I would never choose to have another. I do a lot less of the childcare than L, but I'm not too bad.
>
> When you become a parent, your life takes on the role of a carer. By 9 pm you're exhausted. The logistics of life get so complicated. Parenthood brings back a regimentation to your life that you thought you'd escaped at 18. I don't find being a dad much fun – it's tiresome and tedious. We have conversations about buying packs of boy's pants from Primart. L resents the fact that I refuse to have more children which is very heavy. She grieves for the children she is never going to have. I feel under pressure from people who think it's 'cruel' to have an only child. It's not great for our relationship, to say the least.
>
> It's hard to say I regret what I've done with my life because I made a deal. I wish I had met a woman I loved that didn't want children, but there aren't many around.
>
> *M, 56, company director, London*

Little research has been carried out specifically into how men feel about parenthood, but initial findings of a three year Australian Government survey[1] show more than a quarter of young men don't expect to have children – slightly more than their female peers. The survey's project director thinks young men are concerned about the lifestyle consequences of having children, which correlates with results showing that parents of young children are less satisfied with their lives than childless couples. Canadian research reflects this trend.[2]

An old girlfriend who wanted children told me I was an immature commitment-phobe. Her words stung because I think my reasons for not wanting children are well thought through. It's true that I don't want a lot of responsibilities, but I'm not out drinking and chasing women every night and my decision doesn't harm anyone. That girlfriend hasn't met anyone to have a baby with yet, but I can't be held responsible for that.

Bradley, 39, Toronto

My wife Maggie and I have two lovely children but we both find downsides in being parents. If they're upset I try to cuddle and console them but they always want their mum, which can feel like rejection. On the other hand, my son Laurie treats me like some sort of super-hero at weekends, though it's Maggie who's looked after him and his sister all week. He says, 'Come on Daddy, you and me can go in the spaceship and Mummy can make the sandwiches.' I feel a bit sorry for Maggie. She trained as a barrister and is far cleverer than me.

Duncan, 37, political lobbyist

Some fathers apparently have a knack of turning their key in the lock just as the bedtime story book has been closed and the nursery light switched off. *Time* magazine[3] reported that a mother's love for her child is unconditional, while that of fathers is more qualified and tied to performance. Mothers worry about their children's survival while fathers concentrate on their future achievements. In America, a sample research group of both adults and children was asked to list the categories of people most important in the children's lives.[4] Fathers came third – behind mothers and grandparents and ahead of clergy and ... rabbits.

Modern 'TotalDads' are rare and say they face higher hurdles in their reversed roles than full-time working mothers, because fatherhood is seen as un-macho.

> I am not accepted by mothers who look after their children full-time like I do. There's a clique of them at the park and although we say good morning and the kids run about together, I always end up sitting on a bench reading my newspaper while they chat. I've tried to integrate, but I am not welcome. If I cared more I'd bake some drop scones and offer them round but if they're that small-minded they won't include me willingly, I doubt we'd have much to talk about anyway.
>
> I never liked my job (as a pen-pusher at the council) and Gillian's career was going from strength to strength when we found out she was pregnant. It makes sense for me to look after the kids and I prefer it to my job. I don't know anyone else like me. I have never seen a dad at Tumble Tots during the week, but dads do take their kids swimming at weekends.
>
> Looking after children is no great mystery. We have fun together, I get cross with them sometimes, we have cuddles and tears, and sometimes I get mind numbingly bored. I think I'm better at ignoring them if

they're winding me up than Gillian, though she may disagree. If the kids are pesky I put old clothes on them and stick them in the garden with a load of water or paint. I go inside and watch the cricket or read my book or cook something for supper. We leave each other alone and I certainly don't feel the need to watch over them all the time or jump up every time they cry.

I've heard women say they hate when their husband comes home and they're still dressed in a top that's got mashed banana smeared over it. I don't understand why they make such a big deal of it. It takes seconds to take off one shirt and put on another (and yes, I do iron them).

The most prejudiced incident that happened was when I was on the bus one day with Jacob. Two women sitting behind me called the conductor over and told him he should ask 'where that man at the front got that child.' The conductor recognised me and Jacob – it's our usual route – so he gave me a wink. It was on the number 35 on Gresham Road in Brixton. I'll never forget it.

John, father of two, London

Until the early 1800s childrearing manuals were not addressed to mothers but to fathers. The class system was entrenched and in wealthy society it was a patriarchal era. Becoming a father assured esteemed status, though a man was judged by the money he earned and not on his nurturing ability. In working-class families, however, roles were often reversed. In the north of England cotton spinning jennies provided work for thousands of women – the original spinsters – who earned a living for their families while the menfolk stayed home.

Songs for the Nursery, 1805

Hush thee my babby,
Lie still with thy daddy,
Thy mammy has gone to the mill.
To grind thee some wheat
To make thee some meat,
Oh, my dear babby, lie still.

In the rare instances of marital separation a father's custody of children was unlikely to be questioned. By the 20th century however, women were generally considered best primary custodians. Modern fathers are awarded charge of their children in fewer than ten per cent of cases after divorce, it's reckoned[5] and many have limited rights of access. Some feel deeply discriminated against because of this, and campaigning groups – notably Fathers-4-Justice in the UK – have resorted to direct action to try to remedy the situation. Plenty of other fathers disappear and avoid paying maintenance for their children. It is simply not possible to generalise about men's attitudes towards children – their own or other people's.

Situations in which one half of a couple wants children and the other doesn't appear to be resolved differently around the world. Data shows that in the more likely (but not guaranteed) scenario where the male is the reluctant partner, American couples are more likely to end up without children than in Europe, where women usually succeed in talking their man around.[6]

I never want to have a child. I mean, I like kids, but I do not think I want to have one (or more) for myself. I have this thinking since very young age, probably 12 or 13, and never change my mind since. However I am from Asian heritage where people are conservative. Most can't accept and do not respect my decisions, including friends and family. I am together with my boyfriend for four years, now the problem is, he wants kids and I do not. I told him about my decision and he just said I will change my mind. My boyfriend has proposed to me two times, but I say no because he still refuse to accept that I'm a childfree. We are loving but we just can't agree on this topic. You may have wise advice perhaps?

I wish he was like your husband, Nicki. Seriously if he would support my decision I will immediately marry him. But he just keep saying 'you will change, trust me I am right'. It is so good to know there are people like you who feel the same way as I do. Other questions people ask is:

'Who is going to take care of you when you are old?'

'You are not complete until you give birthday.'

'What about your parents, they will feel lonely without grandchilds'.

Just the other day a married colleague asked me, 'How many kids you plan to have?' I say 'none' and his jaw was dropping.

Jaclyn, 26, engineer, Kuala Lumpur, Malaysia

Jerry Steinberg
founder of No Kidding!, the International Social Group for Childfree People
b 1945

My reasons for not wanting children of my own are numerous and varied. Of course, I have environmental concerns, because I believe that most – if not all – of the world's problems result from overpopulation: pollution of air, water, land, noise and light; depletion of natural resources; crime, disease, war, famine. I feel a sense of social responsibility by not breeding.

I have other priorities in my life that would be precluded by having children: I like knowing that I am Number One with my wife, and she's Number One with me and I absolutely cherish having the freedom to enjoy my life. I work part-time teaching English as a second language. It doesn't pay enough to support a family, but it's extremely enjoyable and rewarding. I love to come home to a quiet or a noisy house – whatever I choose. I can put on loud music if I'm in the mood, or sit quietly with a book. I watch what I want on TV (not hours of children's shows!) and I'm spontaneous in my activities. It's wonderful to go for a walk at midnight with my wife, spend half an hour on the beach with the dogs or meet a friend for lunch with half an hour's notice without having to plan days ahead and make arrangements for a babysitter. After work I am free to come home from work and relax rather than having to drive Child A to his/her soccer game, pick up Child B from piano lessons, take Child C to his/her friend's house across town, etc; My wife and I can buy whatever car we like or live without one, and we can live in any house in any neighbourhood without having to take into account proximity to, and quality of, elementary and high schools in the area.

It's a pleasure to chat on the phone with a childfree friend for half an hour, without interruptions (such as, 'I want some ice cream!' or 'Can Kim stay for supper?' or 'Make Chris stop picking on me!' or 'Where's my skateboard?'). I can wake up early or sleep-in late as I wish or need to. All these examples are simple pleasures that I never take for granted. They all add up to FREEDOM!

I have limited patience with children; in other words, I enjoy them for a time, then I yearn to be away from them and in a peaceful place. People who don't know me assume that I must not like children if I don't want any, while friends and relatives know that I do like children, and that I get along very well with children. I have been asked on radio phone-in shows how I can say that I like kids when I don't want any. Once I responded, 'I am also quite fond of breasts, but I don't want any!'

Chapter 9
Sanctimonious Parents

All you need in life is ignorance and confidence;
then success is guaranteed.
Mark Twain

A group of colleagues are sharing an after-work drink in a pub near the BBC's Broadcasting House. It's the day of the ending of the Beslan siege in Russia, in which hundreds of people, many of them children, were killed. An obnoxious woman among us pipes up: 'Of course, you can only understand the true pain of those people if you're a mother yourself.' In my ears the clink of wine glasses is replaced by the baa of spring lambs in a field. Sometimes even normally outspoken journalists behave like sheep. The woman holds court to nods of agreement until my friend Lucy takes on the role of farmer with his gun. Her vocal shot silences the noise in mid-bleat and Lucy makes clear in a furious and steely voice that no one is ever to suggest again that not having children makes her less capable of human compassion. The bleating begins again, this time in Lucy's favour.

In a newspaper article captioned 'Big Breasts, Low IQ and a Personality Bypass – The Awful Truth About Life After A Baby',[1] a laudably honest reporter wrote that she can't help feeling smug as she queues in the supermarket as part of a middle-class couple, with a beautiful baby and a trolley full of organic vegetables. Women who've done something unremarkable often consider themselves enigmatically special, but smugness is rarely visible on the face of unique achievers. Caught in the light of the snappers' flashbulbs, for example, double-gold Olympian Kelly Holmes looked delighted, certainly; over-awed, for sure; but smug? No.

One mum I arranged to interview asked ME more questions than I asked her:

> You are the first person I've met who doesn't want to have children. I find it hard to understand because you're missing out on an extra dimension to life. Your decision is fascinating because it's so conscious. Most people don't analyse whether or not to have a baby. They think 'oh, as and when' and end up pregnant somehow, sometime. They fall into it. But to have that very strong feeling you don't want children must mean there is a very strong reason behind it. You say you like to be with your husband and there is that saying that 'the children of lovers are orphans'. There's some truth in that, I think. Every woman has to choose between their baby and their husband because you're

dividing your time more, but in the end I feel it's enriching. But I can't believe that's your real reason? Perhaps you don't think you'd be a very good mother?

If you are never going to worry about anybody you might as well live in a cave. Why have a relationship? You must worry about your husband? Caring about other people is a good thing and those that don't care are isolated, damaged and unable to relate to other human beings. You don't know that your child will be sad or bullied. You live a more free life than I do, but you're cutting off the chance to experience something and that seems very self-limiting to me. Why do you think you would be so unable to bend? Your priorities would just change as they do anyway as you get older. You won't hold on to your Mexico moment forever.

You have a busy job, but you could scale down. I have a job and children! Maybe you could have the confidence to say that you're not going to try to do everything, because otherwise you're missing out on a lot of fun.

I'm not saying you're unfulfilled but you are consciously saying that you don't want to experience something. It's like saying, 'I am never going to go out and get a job,' to which I'd say, 'Why not? It's fun and interesting, your brain gets stimulated, you meet other people and it leads to other things.' You're cutting yourself off from opportunity. Having your own children could be dreadful but it could be joyous and wonderful.

> If you don't feel personally right for it for whatever reason, I wouldn't say you really should have children. Don't rule it out though, you might decide you want a baby in a couple of years.
>
> *Rosemary, 49, mother of four*

Later that evening, as is routine, I phoned Rosemary to thank her for meeting and to check a few details. The answerphone was on so I left a message after the high moral tone.

When Jim and I got married, instead of a wedding list we asked friends who wanted to bring us a gift for a copy of their favourite book of all time. Our presents ranged from *The Cat in The Hat* through numerous novels to a Japanese love story and a hardback of photographs from Southern Asia. A science correspondent friend gave us Tom Wolfe's *The Right Stuff*, a novel about the American/Russian space race. Wolfe describes perfectly how some women, especially, bask in the reflected glory of other people and believe that their own status is raised as a result:

> **The classic and often told story of service wives concerned the wives of a group of Navy pilots who had just been transferred to a new base. A commander designated to give the wives an orientation lecture says: 'First would you ladies please rearrange yourselves by rank, with the highest-ranking wives sitting in the first row and so on back to the rear.' It takes about fifteen minutes for the women to sort themselves out and change their seats, since very few of them know one another. Once the process has been**

> **completed the commander fixes a stern glare upon them and says: 'Ladies, I want you to know that I have just witnessed the most ridiculous performance I have ever seen in my entire military career. Allow me to inform you that no matter who your husbands are, you have no rank whatsoever. You are all equals and you should kindly remember to conduct yourselves as such in all dealings with one another.'**
>
> *from* The Right Stuff *by Tom Wolfe*

There are mothers who do exactly the same with their children. They wear them, like badges. Some have told me they feel personally slighted if an invite to a wedding excludes their children, and some admit declining such invitations in a fit of pique. But if 20 couples were to bring two kids each, the numbers and costs would escalate beyond most hosts' budget.

On the day of the London Marathon, six of us traipsed up to Tower Bridge in the pouring rain to cheer on the bedraggled charity runners as they reached the killer cobbles at mile 24. The Metropolitan Police consider the event the biggest day of the year for crowd control – more than a million spectators usually line the route. Tower Bridge, being a famous landmark, is the most popular vantage point. We wanted to cross to the north side, but a policeman with his radio to his ear explained in a stern monotone that there was gridlock on the bridge – caused by a double buggy. He made us wait a few minutes before allowing us to wriggle forward shoulder to shoulder with the rest of the crowd. Halfway across we bumped into the mum with the double buggy, which was as wide as the pavement. She was formidable – like Boudicca with her chariot – and her demeanour declared that the congestion was everyone's problem but hers. One hand on the buggy, the other on her hip, she tutted impatiently as dozens of spectators snagged their Gore-Tex on the barricades and apologised *to her* as they clambered by.

Is it the everyday hassle of transporting young kids around town that causes delusions of grandeur in women who push buggies? Those who take their bikes on the tube have no problem doing so courteously and I've never witnessed anyone in a wheelchair demanding space with the same self-righteous entitlement that some mothers do. Only buggies (and urban buggies are worse) carry the misplaced sense of superiority, and it's because? They've got *children* in them. At next year's marathon the VIP Mum will probably demand her own roadblock and police escort.

> What I hate is the culture at the moment that implies that children are virtually sacred and, by association, so are parents. It's almost a quasi-religious thing! Children used to be part of a family, now they're the centre of it and everything revolves around them.
>
> *Alex, 41, civil servant, London*

A while ago I was on a crowded tube train when an elderly man got on. Three adjacent seats were occupied by a mother and her two robust looking children. The man remained standing, but unsteadily, directly in front of them. Before long another passenger intervened on his behalf and suggested to the mother that one of her kids swap places with him. Her posture changed like an off-guard cat bumping into a dog. Back arched, hackles up – relaxed to defensive in a single movement that somehow manages to be slow and swift at the same time. 'My children are tired,' she declared in the manner of Miss Jean Brodie. 'They deserve to sit down as much as anyone else.' The boy, who was about 12, had already begun to stand, but his mother told him to stay where he was. Someone else gave up their seat for the man and the journey continued, the children squirming in embarrassment as nearby passengers embarked on a hushed debate about selfishness that was really quite animated for the Northern Line.

There is the excuse that women take maternity leave from high-powered jobs and are simply being assertive when it comes to the needs of their children, but it's not assertiveness that's on display.

Sanctimonious: making a show of piety.
Pious: hypocritically virtuous.
Assertive: forthright, positive.

OED

It is no achievement to have a baby, anyone can have sex! Raising a child to be a responsible adult, now that is an achievement, but not one that can be claimed when the child is sitting in a pushchair. I can understand congratulations are in order when a woman has delivered a baby, but people send cards when someone gets pregnant. One of the reasons I decided to remain childfree was because I realised I'd never be 'just me' again and I didn't want that.

Orla, 48, ornithologist

Sanctimonious mothers (and those that insist on telling you how bright their children are) undermine the genuine importance of their role. Much of the language that surrounds motherhood has the same effect and is exclusive to women. Most of us, whether or not we have children, slip instinctively into baby talk when communicating with infants. But mothers who continue to use it in adult conversation damage their self-respect. The afore-mentioned *Preggie-Pops* are just the beginning. *Yummy Mummy* has a rather desperate ring to it when, at the same time, mothers continually refer to themselves as '*just* Lucy's mum' or '*just* a taxi-driver' if the children are teenagers. Fathers rarely describe themselves as just anything, unless they're joking. One mum told me that baby language for adults drives her mad too. 'If my antenatal teacher had referred to breast milk as "the ultimate fast-food" one more time,' she said, 'I'd have thumped her.'

I'm intrigued by Baby on Board stickers in cars. There are usually plenty in sight when you're stuck in traffic. A recent one I spotted displayed a version with the additional wording 'please be patient,' as though the infant itself was at the wheel. If Baby on Boards are a harmless display of pride, why pretend that they're anything else? But some parents, in a game but bizarre argument, will try to convince you they're necessary and purposeful – providing an instant signal to emergency services that a child might be trapped in a crash. Others I've spotted read 'Twins on Board' or even 'Small Person on Board' – perhaps for the myopic fireman. Do parents really take the trouble to remove the stickers if they use the car when the kids aren't in it? What if one of the twins goes for a ride but the other stays home? If motorists believe that other motorists will drive more safely around a car with a baby in it, perhaps we should all have a Baby on Board car-sticker, regardless of whether we actually have a baby.

London Underground has recently begun issuing Baby on Board badges for pregnant women to pin on their coats. The idea is that other passengers will be encouraged to let them sit down, without risking the embarrassment of offering a seat to a woman who looks pregnant, but isn't. The idea's caused great amusement, but it in fact makes much more sense than a car sticker. Pregnant women are more comfortable sitting down - so there's a valid reason for wearing this badge.

I asked a police officer how many lives have been saved by the presence of Baby on Board stickers and he didn't believe I was genuinely trying to validate something I'd heard.

> I call it the Utter Sanctity of Parenthood and it bores me to death. If I see a child I might think he or she is nice, but it doesn't mean I want one.
>
> *Alison, London*

Steve Broomfield was a pillar of the community in his local village, until he fell victim to sanctimonious parent power at the summer fete he'd played a key role in organising. I read about him in a regional newspaper.[2] Steve accidentally made a comment over the public address system on the day of the fete, not realising that it was live and could be heard by all the spectators. Glancing at the schedule for the day, he groaned as a parade of toddlers on quad bikes bumped their way into the main arena. 'Oh no, not the bike kids again,' he went on, 'they're crap.' Such was the outrage among parents at the fete that Steve was forced to make a public apology, pay a donation to a charity (of the bike kids' choice! – average age five) and resign from the carnival committee on which he'd worked voluntarily for the last ten years.

Once, on the hottest day of the year, I queued for ice creams in Hyde Park with a little girl wearing pink Wellington boots and a spotty raincoat. Her mum told me despairingly she just couldn't get her to put on her dress, and I admired her daughter's independent spirit. It's one thing likewise for swashbuckling pirates and Spidermans to accost you in the supermarket on a Saturday morning, but when the subjects of sartorial ignominy are too small to have had any say in the matter I feel sorry for the way they're paraded around. Dressing up chimps as tea ladies and getting circus animals to ride bicycles is considered a bit humiliating these days, but parents think nothing of adorning their kids in panda-eared jump suits and pushing them up high streets in pink plastic Barbie cars. On holiday one time Jim and I kept bumping into a Canadian couple on a tandem whose toddler was encased in a large yellow trailer, emblazoned with a maple leaf, that they pulled along behind them. He seemed about as dignified as a mollycoddled king in a sedan chair.

All this idolatry is better than those parents who moan about their children and seem so incessantly burdened by the hardships of their role that you wonder why they bothered in the first place but, just once, it would be nice to open a round-robin letter one Christmas that gives a realistic update of a family's ups and downs throughout the year: 'Jennifer failed her A Levels' perhaps, or 'Daniel's doing well in the Young Offender's Institution'. My favourite letter read like a press release and crowed how a child had 'successfully won' the school English Prize. A gift evidently not inherited from the parent who wrote it.

'It's a Family Affair'
by Julie Bindel
Guardian, 7 February 2004

I knew it was bad news when my mum rang me at the office. She said there was something horrible about me in the newspaper, so bad that she'd hidden it from dad. Imagining that it was yet another men's rights group insisting that women have it all their way, I reassured her, saying this was the name of the game when you say things that offend. But no, it was a column slagging me off because I'd said something I never thought would cause such offence: I had dared to suggest, in this newspaper, that women would be better off not having children and that if the government wanted to help us live a better quality of life, it should pay us a bonus for remaining childless.

All hell broke loose! Not only did I have some columnist calling me a bitter, man-hating lesbian, I had friends asking if I really said those awful things, 'because lots of women will be really upset'. Diddums! I was evil for criticising breeding, and had broken the golden rule: never question what one friend called 'the sunshine miracle of motherhood'. The emails came dripping in – vitriol like I had never seen – including one from an infertile woman who likened me to Hitler for 'wanting to phase out the human race'.

It was only then that I realised I did not hate children. I didn't have a road to Damascus conversion and start gazing in Mothercare windows; I just realised that the irritation I feel when forced into a space with them is towards the parents. Don't get me wrong: I don't like kids. They're boring, troublesome and, especially if they have been brought up by middle-class tosserati in north London, precocious. My venom, however, is reserved for the smug parents who literally behave as if the world owes them a favour, and believe they should commandeer respect for simply having children.

Yesterday, I was on a bus in rush hour on my way to earn enough money to pay tax to keep other people's children in education and child benefit. Suddenly, an elderly woman sitting in a priority seat was knocked flying when a smug mum pushed her way on with one of those three-wheel monster pushchairs, made for walking over rough terrain but used in Crouch End for nipping out for a latte. No one complained except me, and then I was looked at as if I had picked up the baby and eaten it.

What upsets me is the fact that people who choose to bring yet another child into the world get so much more validation, support and access to public resources than those who perform the thankless task of caring for ill, old or disabled dependents. It's a wonder parents don't insist on pushchair lanes so they don't have to be bothered with childless pests on the pavements. In my local Starbucks, I regularly get stuck in a queue waiting until little Ollie decides he wants a double woca choca latte frappe, and do the muffins contain gluten? Last Sunday, a customer lit up near the brood. He'd have got less of a reaction if he'd waved his willy around.

Judging by the amount of moral superiority that oozes from some, you would think that giving birth is akin to curing cancer, and therefore makes parents entitled to special treatment. Those in traditional family units are allowed paternity and maternity leave, automatic benefits, instant access to specialist medical care, tax relief and gushing admiration from the public. They are allowed to board flights first, have 'family friendly' carriages on trains and jump the queue at doctors' surgeries. Try being a carer for an adult with mental health problems and notice the difference – you have to beg for intervention, wait years for benefits and, if you complain about the stress it causes, you are asked, 'Why do it in the first place?', as if every caring role, apart from parenthood, is a choice.

Why is it that, in a modern, western society, so many people desperately want their own babies? Some who can't conceive become suicidal at the prospect, and the courts are clogged up with cases about the right to IVF on the NHS and the ownership of sperm.

Lesbians and gays have long known that those with kids are afforded higher status than those without, which is why more and more are now having them. Why endure all the costs and paraphernalia of AID [Artificial Insemination by Donor] or surrogacy to spend the next 18 years chained to the demands of child rearing?

But if that's what you want, why not adopt? Children's homes are full of unwanted babies and toddlers, yet more are being brought into the world at great cost. Child-rearing is seen as a selfless enterprise, but those who choose to give birth to their own cannot argue that they're doing a scrap of good for the world. Look at baby showers, where guests turn up with boxes of Baby Gap before it has even been born. What are we doing, rewarding those who reproduce and put further strain on the world's resources?

If we are to accept that it is a human's innate right to have our own children, we'll continue to find more ways to produce them, whatever the cost. In the meantime, it costs more than £600 a week to keep one child in care. If you want to leave a legacy behind when you die, try campaigning against child neglect. It might keep you awake at night, but at least you won't get sore nipples.

Chapter 10
Free Range Children

It takes a village to raise a child.
African proverb
It takes a child to raze a village.
westernised, updated version

London's Tate Modern, where art is housed in a huge old power station across the river from St Paul's Cathedral, is a popular destination for family outings. The building is vast and airy, but the resulting echoes are not the magnified murmurs of an appreciative public, but the shrieks and foot stomping redolent of a nursery school. A colleague told me over the water cooler one morning of a 'hilarious' visit he and his wife had enjoyed with their two boys, one of whom had clambered onto the life sized exhibits of a new installation.

'Please do not touch the artworks: Even clean hands leave marks and damage surfaces' read the clearly displayed signs on the entrance to every exhibit.

My colleague assumed I'd appreciate the cute antics of his son and was taken aback when I said I agreed with the security guard who scolded the boy. If the child had smeared toffee on the *Mona Lisa* would his reaction have been the same?

I asked a friend what she would do if her three (well-behaved) children ran rampage round an art gallery. 'I'd take them out,' she replied, before adding, 'though I suppose it depends on your definition of rampage.' Childfree people tend to appreciate peace and quiet and prefer the company of children whose parents have explained that different types of behaviour are appropriate for different environments. But few do so and, in addition, those who have children seem to have developed immunity to noise.

The long play version of the soundtrack to the 21st century strikes a lot of people as irritating and superfluous. Somewhere, a salaried person dreamed up Petrol Station Forecourt TV and the Board approved it. In Florida, divers can tune in to the banal prattle of the DJs on Scuba FM, launched to 'enhance' exploring the undersea world. Mobile phones get answered in cinemas and sex lives discussed on public transport. Young men who build powerful speakers into their cars apparently hold a genuine belief that they're 'offering' their music, like missionaries, to the uninitiated.

> I was a quiet child. For as long as I can remember I've enjoyed peace and tranquillity. My parents used to worry that I didn't have enough to keep me occupied but I was always happier listening to the birds singing and the wind whistling than playing noisy games. I have a brother who has children of his own

now, but we're like oil and water. As an adult I like to think my own thoughts, read, study and enjoy nature. There are plenty of places where children can let off steam, but there's nowhere I can go to find silence. Even libraries aren't quiet anymore. Sometimes I think the librarians are too nervous to confront parents of noisy children because they get so huffy. I don't want my own children because I couldn't stand the constant onslaught of sound.

I left school and worked until my late twenties before deciding to go back to university as a mature student. I went home to live with my parents while I was studying. They live on an estate full of family houses. Getting my degree was really important to me and I began to get very tense because I couldn't concentrate on my work when lots of children were playing outside. They were so noisy it was like living in the middle of a school playground. That was the beginning of realising how much I'd hate exposure to that all the time. The noise babies and toddlers make when they're crying or screaming tears through me. High-pitched shouting – even if it's playful – is really intrusive. I also hate the electronic noises that children are fond of like Game Boys, television, Walkmans and all those tunes on mobile phones. Over the years I've got more disillusioned with how intolerant parents are of my point of view.

After I got my degree I went into charity work. I've been able to buy my own house, but my salary limited what I could afford. I live in an area where the properties are very close together. One weekend when I was working from home the two boys from the house opposite came out to play football with their dad in the cul-de-sac we live on. I tried to ignore them but after a while I thought I'd have a word. A week before the dad had knocked on my door and asked if I could turn my security light around because it was shining into one of the children's bedrooms. Of course I did it immediately, so I felt it would be okay to explain that his kids were interrupting my work. It didn't turn out like that. I went outside and asked would they mind being quieter. My tone was friendly enough, but although the dad agreed to take the boys to the other end of the road, he was grudging about it. It was just before Christmas and for the first time in years they didn't put a card through my door. It may have been coincidence but I don't think it was. I got the impression he thought I was making a fuss, criticising even. None of the family acknowledges me anymore.

One weekend the children next door spent hours batting a ball against our adjoining wall. Either they and their parents didn't consider it might be annoying, or they didn't care. I think a lot of parents are so busy and stressed that it's a relief if the children are amusing themselves whatever they're up to. They're immune to the noise their children are generating. I suppose they're just used to it. Another time on a train I asked three boys who were yelling over a game of cards if they could be a bit quieter and their parents told me I should move if I didn't like where I was sitting. The woman in the seat behind sided with them and I found it very humiliating.

I get anxious these days even at the prospect of being disturbed. I think it's because, though I've tried not to moan, on the occasions I've got really fed-up and intervened the response has been hostile. I have no option but to put up with it, which doesn't seem fair. I'm thinking of moving into the centre of the city if I can afford a flat there. It might seem strange, but more generalised, urban noise doesn't bother me. I've been called child-phobic by colleagues who see me getting tense if they bring their children into the office or if we go out for lunch and there are kids running around. I'm prepared to accept I'm ultra-sensitive to the sound children make. I know I'm in a minority. But I feel hurt that all I crave is peace and quiet. I don't disturb anyone else, but I'm the one who is considered miserable and intolerant.

Eileen, 45, academic

The satirical magazine *Private Eye* runs a cartoon in each issue titled 'Scenes You Seldom See'. One was a pen and ink drawing of a woman sitting outside a church with a howling baby on her lap. 'He won't stop crying so I've brought him out of the service,' ran the caption.

At a wedding I went to last summer, the lamentably rare opportunity to sing 'Dear Lord and Father of Mankind' in a very loud voice was interrupted by a small boy running up the aisle after the bride and groom. His parents nudged each other and smiled indulgently before reluctantly taking steps to retrieve him. Friends who visited the Sistine Chapel when their first baby was small related rather guiltily how he'd screamed his head off throughout the guided tour. 'What were we supposed to do?' they asked, when we talked about it. 'Have one of us take him outside while the other enjoyed the visit?' Er ... yes, would have been my answer if I'd been bold enough to be honest, which I wasn't. It's one of the downsides of children.

Toys that bleep and squeak are not satisfactory instruments of calm.

Some parents don't realise their children are being annoying (never is love so blind as when the object of one's affection is clothed in BabyGap), and some don't care.

'They're so sweet – they had a chat with everyone in the cafe,' parents have told me with pride and delight. And I've thought mmm ... not so marvellous for the customer seeking solitude with his cappucino.

> I just returned home after working in London for a few years. One of my jobs was as a waitress at a smart restaurant on the Strand. Sunday brunch was popular with the rich, busy set and they would all arrive and meet up with their friends. But it was not a family morning out. The parents wanted the time to themselves and paid no attention to the children from the moment they walked inside. The kids ran riot. They sat at the table for a maximum of ten

> minutes to eat their food, and it's the only time their parents spoke to them in two or three hours.
>
> *Sioban 30, Warrnambool, Australia*

Children are boisterous by nature and you'd have to be pretty mean-spirited to want to deny that. The problem lies with adults who have little respect for the others they're sharing their space with.

Lots of public spaces, galleries in particular, have great facilities in the way of family rooms and workshops dedicated to kids, but parents don't want to use them. Why spend time joining the dots to create a Picasso when the real one is just down the corridor?

The high population density of UK cities makes the situation more volatile. In Washington (where I spent a week covering a Presidential election whose outcome seemed largely dependent on which candidate could 'kill bad guys' fastest) I surprised myself. In the few hours before my flight home I went to an exhibition of Islamic art in the vast, relatively empty National Gallery. The first sound I heard when I walked down the escalator was a baby's wails and it didn't bother me at all. Instead my kneejerk reaction was: 'Thank God that people are bringing their children here.'

Designated childfree and child-friendly days at arts venues are beginning to be mooted and could solve the problem of differing requirements.

> **I welcome it when efforts are made to accommodate children in museums. However, it would be nice if**

they started considering childfree days too when there are not hordes of small people fluttering around.

Roy Strong, former director, National Portrait Gallery and the V&A, London

But segregation seems such a victory for intolerance.

> Being a good parent involves sacrificing what you want to do to accommodate what the children can manage – it's the bottom line. But increasingly these days, parents want their own lives to continue as they were before they had the kids, which is unrealistic. Mine are grown-up now, but I was strict about bringing them up. My husband and I ate in restaurants far less when they were small, until they learned to sit still – and if we did go into a museum, the children understood it was a grown-up place.
>
> *Magda, 50, Portsmouth*

When it comes to non-criminal, low level disturbance, parents turn a blind eye towards the behaviour of other people's children as well as their own. Nobody has to take responsibility for what kids get up to because there'll always be back-up - it's how majority rule works. It's only (and rarely) people without kids who are prepared to confront a disruptive family in a public setting. They are then attacked for interfering – often (to prove the point) not just by the family in question, but by other families standing nearby.

Even a tactful intervention about unreasonable behaviour is akin to slagging off Mother Teresa. It's another anomaly that while parents see fit to have opinionated views on being childfree, non-parents are immediately discredited if they comment on any aspect of child-rearing. Waitresses get scowled at for asking parents if their children might play away from other tables and a colleague who asked to change seats on an aeroplane after being consistently kicked in the back by the child behind him, was verbally abused by the whole family, who were travelling together. He got the indignant 'well, you obviously haven't got kids' riposte that's used in the context of an excuse, though it's neither here nor there.

My airline steward friend asks inconsiderate parents if their children would like to play outside.

Childfree people get told they should lighten up, but there are pernicious problems with a lack of basic courtesy which children would ideally learn from their parents. In the summer term of 2003, ten children a day were excluded from schools in England and Wales[1] for assaulting a teacher or another pupil. Such behaviour can translate into adult aggression. In the same time period, some schools excluded more parents from their premises than they did children. Three out of four American teenagers told researchers they believe violent behaviour is learned. Of those, 43 per cent said it's picked up from parents; 20 per cent blame television.[2] Their conclusions are in keeping with an earlier academic study in which researchers concluded that children imitate life rather than art – television being less to blame for copycat aggression than the influence of adults around them.[3]

Anti-Social Behaviour Orders weren't heard of when we were kids. There was anti-social behaviour, but it wasn't a matter for the courts. Signs that read 'Our Staff Have A Right to Carry Out Their Work Without The Threat Of Violence' used to be confined to night buses and job centres, but lately one's appeared in our local Greggs the Bakers.

Parents have a blinkered assumption that everyone finds their children as endearing as they do. Whenever I bump into the lady next door she tells me how wonderfully musical her children are, as if I didn't know. Victorian terraces do not have thick walls; one plays the clarinet, another the trumpet and the youngest is learning the drums. I have heard parents say that they are just too tired to care what their children get up to as long as they're safe. Others just shrug and say, 'What can you do?' even if their children are awful. I have a friend who's a single dad and I feel sorry for him because he's struggling with his daughter. When he tries to discipline her she cries for her mum which makes him really upset, so he backtracks and says that he's sorry. It's sad because then he feels bad about giving conflicting signals.

I don't think children are overindulged though. Society has demonised them and older people treat all young people as though they are yobs. I respect young people more than most parents. I think many adults are tricked into thinking they have to have kids and either become resentful or just can't cope with

> the amount of energy it takes. People think my own decision not to have children is either a reflection of my level of commitment to my own work or that working with challenging young people has put me off having children of my own. Neither is the case.
>
> *Karen, 27, youth worker, Nottingham*

By the side of the ovoid glass headquarters of the London Mayor, a temporary exhibition was set up last summer showing the photographer Tom Stoddart's harrowing images of war, famine and poverty. The pictures were mounted on each face of a square stone pillar, there were about forty in all, and passers-by mingled among them, often standing to stare for an overly long time at a particular image that had stirred them. The evening I was browsing, the atmosphere was fittingly quiet and melancholy, until three energetic children came racing through the statues shouting at the tops of their voices and began using them for a game of hide and seek. The game went on while their father took his time looking around the exhibition. The children were too young to have understood the poignancy of the images on display, but would it have been unreasonable for their father to have taken them to one side, perhaps shown them a few of the photographs, and asked them to play their game on the adjacent grass?

Dismissing unchecked intrusion into other people's lives is a bit like witnessing a scene of rape and pillage and remarking that 'boys will be boys'.

Of course there is a counter argument that further highlights the complexity of family and non-family life and shows how quick we all are to judge each other. For their part, parents feel criticised if their children simply behave like children on occasion.

> Sometimes, although I do my utmost to teach them good manners, my children do misbehave, and then life seems very unfair. You can be in the supermarket, holding on to them and trying to unpack the trolley. They'll be screaming or knocking things off the counter. You're sweating buckets and it feels like a thousand disapproving eyes are watching you. Nobody takes into account that you may not have slept for a week. Every other customer is tut-tut-tutting as though their own children are perfect little angels all the time.
>
> *Helena, London*

Childfree people, however, might be fighting a losing battle. Preaching about the poor behaviour of our youth is perennial.

> **What is happening to our young people? They disrespect their elders, they disobey their parents. They ignore the law. They riot in the streets inflamed with wild notions. Their morals are decaying. What is to become of them?**
>
> ***Plato (427–347 BCE)***

Catherine Tanvier
tennis professional
b 1965

I had a mad life. When I was 15 I was Europe's youngest tennis professional. I played all the major tournaments and was French Number One when I was 17. Tennis has moved on in 20 years but when I was young it was crazy. I was really the first very young woman on the professional circuit. I was in a highly competitive adult world and I travelled all over the world – often alone. By the time Steffi and now Sharapova began to do it there was much more support, but for me there was little. It was very confusing and destabilising. I still try to recover from it.

Partly my reason for not wanting children is related to that time.

To have children you must be stable and able to support them and I don't feel that. You also need the right father and most men do not share equally. The women play the doubles – both partners. They do everything and the men do what they want. Some women will have a baby whatever their circumstances. I am amazed how many tell me they would not be living with their partner if he was not the father of their children. To live with the wrong man! For me that price is too high.

If the marriage breaks it is always harder for the woman. She usually keeps the children and she must find a job to support them. I would not want to work eight hours a day and then have children to look after. Where is there room to be a woman yourself?

I've been lucky to have a gift that has fulfilled me. I don't need a baby and I have seen what families can be like.

My mother was the most beautiful mother, but for many years she had no life as a woman in her own right. After 18 years of marriage my father left when I was 14 and my mum had to bring up us four children alone. There was no financial help from my father. I was just turning professional and I paid for our family – my mum, two brothers and sister. To me the men can do what they like – have children – leave them, and the woman is left to struggle alone. Now my father wants to be in touch and I reject him. He was not a father. I am now the age he was when he left us and I would never behave like that.

My mum became a whole person around this time when he left and also she became my manager. Before then she felt she had no identity and wished she had something for herself. Although it was tough she was happy – travelling to the tournaments with me and arranging everything. For the first time she had a job that was not just looking after children. But it divided our family because her attention was on me. My mother has died now and also my dearest brother. The damage between us all was not repaired. I do not want a life like my mother had.

I have many close friends who are single like me and not wanting children. Women who do have children are suspicious of us. For some I think it is a shock for them to realise they could have thought harder and made a decision not to have children. Others say they needed to have a child. I am not against having children. If I don't have them there is room for someone else to have them instead. I do not care if women think I am socially unconventional. My unusual life has made me strong. I know how to be alone and I have a big curiosity so I will find things not to be bored.

I don't think the world is the right place to bring up children. Adults say, 'Go and watch TV while I have my coffee and cigarette.' Children need more than this. In France there are more than 30 children in each class in school. Within a few years there will be more than 40

in each class. This isn't right. The teachers are not good and the children are not good either. There is too much pressure and it would not be nice to be a child now. Children need two parents to share the commitment – it doesn't matter if it is a man and a woman or a gay couple of either sex, but two are needed.

There are many beautiful children who need love and care. They do not need to be my own blood. I grew up in Nigeria and I would like to go to Africa and work with children there.

We all carry doubt. I have wondered about having children, but my personal situation is not right and nor is the situation in the world. C'est la vie.

Chapter 11
Honest Parents

Having children was the best thing I ever did in my life. And the worst.
Penny, Lancashire

There is, apparently, such a thing as a Positive Birth Experience, though my own friends' stories of bringing their children into the world might easily be narrated by James Herriot. ('She so over-shared,' a friend told me with distaste after visiting a mutual colleague and her new baby in hospital.) Many women feel angry and let down that nobody told them the awful truth about what they'd go through. The conspiracy of silence continues long after labour pains are forgotten. For many, motherhood is the right choice, but for others – usually those who've led previously independent lives – the shock of change is tangible and permanent. Yet there are no dissenters in parenthood – rather like there are no gay footballers.

> Admitting that children are a mixed blessing is the last taboo. Occasionally I have made even a small joke about not liking to be a mum sometimes, and people have been very shocked.
>
> *M, 34, Denmark*

A one-sided, positive presentation of parenthood in which even the unhappy stories are given the 'but it was worth it' gloss, is unhelpful for those people who are thoughtfully considering whether it's for them. The stories that follow are not sensationalist or worse case scenarios, but the testimonies of ordinary men and women who are getting on with their lives, having discovered through bitter experience what a tough commitment parenthood can be.

> I was never crazy about kids but I didn't dislike them. I don't remember a time when I thought I might not have kids. I got married, had a son who is now five and a daughter who is now three. Sounds perfect, right? Wrong. I hate being a parent. I hate being Mommy. My kids are okay people, even cute sometimes, but I don't feel any great love for them. I take good care of them, I'd do everything I could to help them and protect them, but if I had a chance to go back in time, I would not have these children. You're probably expecting some horror story. There isn't one, other than that every day of my life, I wish I did not have children. I wish these children had been born to a mother who could love them. I hate the pressures and expenses of parenthood. The

rewards seem so *few*, *far* between, and not long lasting. The people I know who seem really happy to be parents also seem like they live entirely *for* and through their kids. I can't and won't do that. I *feel* like I'm not my own person any more. Even my husband thinks I'm Mommy, not his *wife*. I've been through counselling and I'm taking antidepressants. I'm not depressed or upset about anything else in my *life*, and a lot *of* times I *feel* happy. Then one *of* the kids gets hurt or it's time to take them to school or day care or they're *fighting* with each other or they don't want to brush their teeth and the cloud *of* unhappiness rains on me again.

I have kids that many people would enjoy being parents to but I simply don't like parenthood. I only hope that will change as they become older and more *self-sufficient*. It's like being in a job you dislike, a job that bores you, that sucks your soul out, except you can't leave this job and go home. It's always there waiting *for* you, needing to be done. This is not the kind *of* thing people like to talk about or admit to themselves or anyone else. I just hope anyone else out there who *feels* the way I do will read this, not *feel* so alone and know that there is at least one other person who is counting down the days until the kids leave home and *life* seems worthwhile again. I guess this is what happens when people have kids without really thinking about whether they truly want to become parents.

S, 40, New Jersey, USA

> I really wanted to have children and I planned how it all would be: picnics on the beach in summer, all of us curled up by a big log fire in the winter. There has been the odd perfect moment but so rarely that I feel cheated. Children can be very divisive in a relationship. I gave up my job, and my social circle that I used to love changed beyond recognition. I look back at my life before I became a mother and I simply cannot believe how good it was. I'm cross with myself that I didn't realise it at the time because those days will never come back. I don't miss wild parties and getting drunk with my single friends, but I miss the carefree feeling that's been replaced by a feeling of duty and I miss the honesty we had with each other about our problems and the things we found hard in life. You can't complain about your children the way you complain about a job or a boyfriend. I knew nothing of this tiredness that never goes away. I used to look at frazzled mothers in the supermarket and think 'I'll never be like that' – but I used to envy them. Now I look at happy, pregnant young women and I think 'you've no idea how your life is about to change'.
>
> *I, 34, Norwich*

In 1975 Esther Lederer, writing as the Chicago based Agony Aunt Ann Landers, received a letter from a young couple undecided about having a baby. They asked her to conduct a survey of her readers that asked whether parents among them would have had children if they'd known what it would be like. The column was syndicated across the US and had a wide circulation. The seventies was an unsettled time for American parents with many young men embroiled in an unpopular war. But at the same time the American Dream – motherhood, apple pie and all – was emerging as an attainable concept for everyone. The survey gained a lot of attention, not only because it was unique for its time but because 70 per cent of the respondents answered No to the question.[1] These are a couple of the responses:

> I am 40 and my husband is 45. We have two children under eight years of age. I was an attractive, fulfilled career woman before I had these kids. Now I'm an overly exhausted, nervous wreck who misses her job and sees very little of her husband. He's got a 'friend' I'm sure and I don't blame him. Our children took all the romance out of our marriage. I'm too tired for sex, conversation or anything.

> I've lived for 70 years and I speak from experience as a mother of five. Was it worth it? No ... not one of our children has given us any pleasure. God knows we did our best, but we were failures as parents and they are failures as people.

Now that fertility treatment is becoming available to more people than in the past, parents face greater pressure to insist they're enjoying their role. It would be very hard to admit that a desperately longed for baby was proving tougher to manage than one might have imagined. Often, IVF results in multiple births, so first time parents are thrown into an incredibly demanding situation.

> I didn't get married until I was 42. My husband and I went through several traumatic cycles of IVF until we were successful. We have twin boys who are now 18 months old. I had worked every day for more than 20 years and found being at home with the boys the most immense struggle. But I had no outlet – nobody to talk to at all – about how I wasn't coping. Even my husband and my mother only wanted to hear that I was sublimely happy in my new role as a mother. I felt embarrassed – fraudulent even – because I had made so much fuss about being desperate for a baby. I bottled everything up and became clinically depressed before finally getting help from my GP. She pointed out that there is a downside to IVF as well – but I couldn't possibly have burst the bubble of 'my miracle babies'. I had to hit rock bottom first.
>
> *E, 46, Birmingham*

In a poll of 600 UK parents in 2000,[2] just four per cent said that child-rearing lived up to their expectations, with one in five admitting they were unprepared for the exhaustion and strain on relationships that having children involved. In a further survey of 1,500 couples, five per cent of the men and a third of the women said children had improved their levels of happiness.[3]

I never imagined how colossal and never-ending the responsibility for my daughter would feel and she's nearly 30 now. Every time she gets on a plane, every time she goes for a job interview, every time she meets a new man, my mind is taken up with fearing for her safety and happiness. The thought that I'll never be free of worrying about her, even if I push it to one side for a while, appals me. My daughter is so free, so happy – I want to warn her not to throw it away. But how can I confess that being her mother has a dark side? How can I invalidate my own existence?

M, 60, Exeter, Devon

I am the mother of two children whom I have brought up exactly the same way. They could not be more different. My son, although he went through some difficult times as a teenager, has turned into a great son. My daughter has broken my heart. She is manipulative and a compulsive liar. We have had to put locks on our bedroom door because she steals from us. It hurts so much. We have bought a safe for money and valuables. I would not wish what I am going through on any other parent. I have never done anything so hard as trying to deal with this situation. My daughter is 18 now and I love her with all my heart. I remember how she was when she was a little girl and it tears me apart. I often feel like killing myself, then hope keeps me going for a while.

Z, 48, university lecturer

Parentline Plus is a charity that offers a telephone support network to parents across the UK. The volunteers who answer helpline calls have all been in a parenting role themselves and each has been trained to help others. They take thousands of calls a year from parents in crisis and know all about the more difficult side of parenthood.

> 45 per cent of our calls are from parents struggling with teenagers. The level of aggression from children to their mothers is shocking. Violence from a husband is no longer the last taboo, calls from women who are being beaten by their sons are common and the women feel very ashamed. It can happen to any woman, it's not a class thing, but those who have never thought about themselves and have always put the children first tend to be victims. Often if dad has left the family or is away a lot the teenage boy inherits the power vacuum. He finds his mother irritating, perhaps he sees her as timid or wet, and he abuses her. Daughters can be very abusive too and it's truly awful for the parents. There are some very disempowered women out there. They've little financial control and the male partner often uses that against them. They can't leave because they wouldn't be able to support themselves.
>
> *Helena, volunteer, Parentline Plus*

US research recently reported that domestic abuse increases by 60 per cent during pregnancy.[4] In the UK, health visitors have recently been instructed to ask pregnant women if their partners are violent towards them. Often, abuse is subtle and psychological – the result of a shift in a couple's circumstances. A mother who's given up her job feels her opinions count for less because her partner pays for everything. Her role is undervalued and her confidence erodes to the point that she's unable to stand her ground if he continually puts her down.

In divorce cases, even if the courts recognise a lower paid woman's contribution to family life and award accordingly, the woman is tied forever to the father of her children. She may be financially provided for, but her emotional freedom remains curtailed.

Just 13 per cent of couples describe themselves as 'equally balanced' financially. Three-quarters of them have no dependent children at home.[5]

> Sometimes I put the phone down and I feel sad, depressed and exhausted. Calls from parents whose children are being bullied at school are heartbreaking because they think there must be a way of accessing support and that everything can be sorted out if only they can find out how to go about it properly. But it's not like that. Some schools have a good policy on bullying but others do very little and some children spend their whole childhood having an utterly miserable time. I often feel depressed about parenthood, it is absolutely not for everyone.
>
> I'm a single mum with my own son D, who is 15. He's great, but his dad left when he was two and it has been very hard. D has never been difficult – he's

> lovely in fact, but even when children are good, there's no living your own life. D was one of those incessantly chatty little boys – it sometimes feels like he's talked non-stop for 13 years. I really love him but it is so wearing, to have to continually attend to him. I would never, ever consider having another child and I would never begin a relationship with a man who wanted children. My friends who are single mothers say the same – we can't wait until our kids leave home and we reclaim a bit of our lives.
>
> *Sharon, volunteer, Parentline Plus*

> Occasionally a call will stay with me for years. I remember a young woman phoning one Christmas. She was just about going under. She had no family, no friends and no money. She was living in a bed-sit with two young children and she desperately wanted to make Christmas nice for them, but was terrified of not being able to hold it together. She wanted to be a good mum but she just wasn't coping. She knew her older child was worried about her. I could see a whole future of emotional and psychological difficulties ahead of them all, on top of everything else.
>
> *Liz, volunteer, Parentline Plus*

The volunteers at Parentline Plus have numerous stories of parents who admit that they simply don't like their kids, which is disappointing in the extreme after all the effort they've put in to raising them. Fathers are often unhappy because children don't share their interests or career ambitions. Mothers are hurt when they become independent and make cruelly clear that they don't want to spend time with them.

Volunteer Helena told me about a call she'd taken the morning I visited that bucked a trend. A mother of four girls was having terrible arguments with her youngest, who was different to her sisters. Like their mum, the older girls liked shopping, trying on make-up and talking about boys. But the child in question preferred quoting poetry and doing her homework. 'I can't work her out,' the mother confided. 'She took down the poster of Boyzone I got her and put Emily Dickinson up on her wall. She's so annoying I want to hit her!'

I don't think you are necessarily missing out on something big if you don't become a parent. There are plenty of ways in which you can be involved in the life of a child and we often talk on the Helpline to grandparents, aunts, uncles and friends who look after children.

ND: Is being a parent a lifelong grind?

It is certainly life long! I can remember wondering why my parents still worried about me when I was growing up and becoming independent. My own children are adults now but I still worry about them, because you know them when they are so vulnerable. But maybe we need people who are worrying about us somewhere, caring for us in other words. Working here we tend to hear a lot of

the difficult sides of parenting, but we should celebrate the good things more. Parenthood gives people a sense of achievement and it's rewarding to see your children growing into adults. I find it astounding to look at my grown-up children. I think it's incredible what a big part (my husband and I) played in seeing them on their way.

ND: Do people get swept into having children without really thinking about it?

Some people think very hard about it, others don't think at all. But both options – having children or not – are a step into the unknown. You don't know how the decision not to have children will affect your life any more than the decision to have them. None of us know what's in store.

ND: What are standards of parenting like, generally?

Mixed. We say there are no rules because children come without instructions and parents have to find their own way. Sometimes they phone at their wits end because their children are being so difficult, and only happen to mention toward the end of the conversation that they are in the middle of a nasty divorce. Parents need to acknowledge their own needs before they can be of much use to their children. If you're running on empty you can't give much to anyone else.

ND: Are parents undervalued?

Yes. We hear a lot about children's rights, but parents need support too. Caring roles are not given status in our society.

ND: What do you do if you're on the bus and there's a bunch of obnoxious 12 year olds shouting and swearing?

I move! All sorts of groups can be intimidating. I'm sure that children find groups of adults intimidating too. Children push boundaries, but it's not nice to see too much of it. Sometimes I see children I know behaving badly and it's easier to understand because you realise it's only a part of their behaviour. Bad behaviour gets noticed and good behaviour doesn't. Lots of children are well behaved.

ND: What would you say to someone who was undecided about having children?

I'd say, 'Are you sure you'll like being a parent? Only do it if you're sure.' Think about it and make your own decision, which may be different at 35 to how you felt at 25. While I believe it's a choice whether or not to have children, I might advise younger women not to do anything drastic like have a sterilisation. If you decide not to have children, I think you are making a very rational decision.

Gill Loughran, deputy chief executive, Parentline Plus

Changes of heart are part of the human condition, and though usually it's those who at first think that they don't want children who end up having them, it can work both ways. I have friends who longed for babies in their thirties, but now in their forties feel glad it didn't happen.

Everyone told me about this love affair that begins when your baby is born. Two days after S was born, the feeling hadn't kicked in and I began to feel guilty that I didn't have this overwhelming love for her. I felt cheated too, but I couldn't have admitted it to anyone. My expectations were so high and I was terribly disappointed – I still am in fact. S is 14 now. I grew to love her of course, but gradually. Everyone goes so overboard about the wonders of having children, but I've found it very restricting. I think people need to make themselves feel better because there's no going back once you've brought a child into the world. You give up your own life to live your child's life and although I appreciate we've been lucky not to have any major dramas, I've found it mundane. My husband and I do the suburban thing – everything is fine on the outside but our child is all we have left in common. I would hazard a guess that most marriages are like ours. There have been plenty of happy times, we're not a volatile family and we get along fine. But when I think of the plans I had when I was young, I'd have chosen differently if I'd had a crystal ball. I've felt torn between providing for S's every need and feeling guilty for missing the life I once had. I was an accomplished pianist and I wanted to perform professionally, but it wasn't possible with the demands of a child. S learned the piano until she was nine and then just refused to practise. I don't think she has any idea that I had a talent. It's natural for children to hurt their parents, they grow away from you so they can be adults themselves. But you have all these hopes and dreams that are completely disregarded. If I had never been a mother, I would have wondered what I was missing out on. Now I know what I have missed out on and that's very disillusioning.

K, 51, Surrey

I have three children under six. I love my kids – they are the best thing that happened to me – but I'm trapped in an unhappy marriage now. My wife E is so different to how she was before the boys came along. Our lives are divided and I resent it. She sees me as a provider of money and not much else. Before the children, I earned a little more than E but we felt equal. She did more work in the house and made all our social arrangements (with mutual friends in those days). We had an easy respect for each other. Our first place was small with low mortgage repayments and we had time to spend with each other. We got on well, it was as simple as that. Money was never an issue and we were really very happy. The second pregnancy was twins. With five of us, E wanted to give up her part-time job and move to the country, so for the last five years I've been commuting from Winchester into London every day which takes two hours. I leave the house at 6.30 every morning and get home around 9 pm. I'm knackered. But E has become the sort of woman who wants to 'keep up with the Joneses'. She was never like that, but now she wants an even bigger house. If one of the kids' friends has a party, E wants to throw a better party. If her friends go on holiday twice a year, she wants me to find the money to go on holiday twice a year. The only people we see socially are those she's met through the children and I don't like them. I'm prepared to work hard – I do it for my kids – but I am never good enough. I know it is tiring to be in the company of children all day, but E has plenty of help from her mum. Her days are spent enjoying the children – they go to the National Trust and visit friends and go to the swings. They are my children too, I would love to spend days like these with them but it's rare that I can. I would love E to give me a kiss and say thank you for doing my best, but we are either fighting about one of the children or not speaking, there is always tension now. When I have a pint in the pub, friends and I joke about it. We all say about our wives 'she's not the woman I married', like we're on a sketch show. But we all mean it.

B, 39, Hampshire

Nobody is honest about parenthood, so how are people to make their own judgement? This is the first opportunity I have had to tell the truth as I see it. Please don't think I am trying to put you off – everyone feels differently – but having children has not been 'worth it' for me. I would choose differently

> if I lived my life again. Of course there are rewards, but until you become a parent, you will never imagine the huge significance the most trivial things take on in the lives of small children. You can't avoid the subservience, the washing, the cleaning, the cooking fish fingers and the kids telling you they hate fish fingers as though they hate you. Day after day they call you Silly Mummy – it's all you are to them sometimes – and it makes you want to cry. As a parent you give up your independence and your identity. You get torn in every direction, practically and emotionally. Your husband doesn't think you are sexy any more, you and he differ on childrearing issues and you argue about it. You worry that he loves the children more than he loves you and you feel selfish for it. You are not a person to your children. Even as they grow up they have no interest in the life you had when you were their age. When your daughter turns into a beautiful 14-year-old you feel discarded and obsolete, and then you feel guilty again. But you love them like you never knew you could love anyone. All the time, this unexplainable love is pulling against your rational mind.
>
> *Penny, 53, Lancashire*

A study conducted by Arizona State University[6] tracked nearly 7,000 American spouses over a number of years. The results showed the happiest couples never had children. Most marriages with children went through a dip in satisfaction when the first baby was born and didn't resume the happiness levels of the pre-children years until the children had grown up and left home. Other parents say that their children leaving home was the saddest time in their lives. There are few activities in life that we all unanimously enjoy regardless of our interests and temperament. It seems mad that everyone is supposed to relish the prospect of having children.

Bea Campbell
writer and broadcaster
b 1947

My mother was one of the founders of the Women's Liberation movement. She brought up myself, my younger sister and brother in the hardship of the austerity that followed the Second World War. She referred to motherhood as 'the ultimate sacrifice' and said every mother of her generation was a lone parent.

We lived in the Scottish Borders. My father worked as a labourer and later retrained as a teacher. Mother was a nurse, and after the three of us were born she went back to work. She left the house at 6 o'clock every morning, seven days a week. I looked after the family then, there was never a question of my father taking on the role. It was a patriarchal society and I believe it still is now. Of course there has been some progress; the average father in the 1950s spent 11 minutes a day alone with his children, whereas the average father today spends 44 minutes alone with his. You could say a four-fold increase is good, but 44 minutes a day? It's hardly equality is it?

My mother was dedicated to the idea of motherhood, but there wasn't a choice then – it was longed for and dreaded, but taken as a given. If there had been choice, women would have been mad to take the option. Mothers still live with that impossible contradiction. Even today I believe motherhood guarantees loneliness and penury. Mothers face a crisis of disappointment when they realise their relationship with their partner will never be the same and he'll never do his share of the childcare. Yet they have the limitless joy that children undoubtedly bring. Women cover up the disadvantages of motherhood because nobody wants to feel crap about the man that they're living with. My mother called it 'the grief of motherhood'. There might be lots of features in broadsheet newspapers about 'hands-on Dads', but I believe it's the middle classes who have changed the least. Middle-class fathers buy time and provision for their children. Working-class fathers can't afford to, so it's in those households that attitudes are changing more swiftly and fathers are playing a fairer role.

Men should be viewed as parents rather than providers. My niece had a baby at the same time Cherie Blair gave birth to Leo and the fact the Prime Minister took no paternity leave seemed like a personal insult to her husband. The message Tony Blair sent out was clear: 'I may have a wife who's just had a fourth baby age 45. I know she'll be knackered, but it's not enough for me to stop working.' My niece's husband, as a committed new father, felt betrayed. He had to use his annual leave to be there for the first weeks of his child's life. He says nothing can echo the importance of how he bonded with his baby in that time.

No masculine institution has made any effort to help women by supporting the role of the father. The mother should be placed at the heart of society but instead her role is continually demeaned. The workplace must reflect the seasons of her day, and complement the layout of a child's day.

Young women are being sold a pup. They misguidedly believe that because you can do a science or a woodwork degree, drive a train or run for Parliament, equality has arrived. Feminism is derided in the media as outdated and they think all things will be fair when they become mothers. What a shock when they find out the truth.

Chapter 12
What You Won't Be Missing Out On

You are your choices.
Jean Paul Sartre

The vast majority of childfree people are not rejecting children, they're rejecting parenthood – which, once embarked upon, lasts for a very long time. Given that it's just not possible to do everything in life, we're all missing out on some things – including a few that childfree people are grateful to be excused.

1. Pregnancy Discrimination

The UK Equal Opportunities Commission helpline receives more calls from women facing problems at work because of their pregnancy than on any other subject. Discrimination is no respecter of social status or job type – it can happen to anyone. A first glimpse of disillusion for the would-be working mum is often apparent about three months after conception when she announces her news to the boss. In law an employer must not dismiss a woman because she's pregnant, but she can be let go for an unconnected reason and such coincidences are suspiciously common. An employee announces she's pregnant and an unscrupulous boss shakes his head and says 'funny you should say that, your performance is poor and I'm about to sack you anyway'. At a time when they should be full of cheer and promise, many women feel undermined, miserable and anxious about the future of a job that they've probably invested heavily in for a number of years.

2. Angst

Modern parents are subjected to a plethora of unsolicited advice. There may be little on offer for the uncertain, but once you take the plunge and have a baby it's impossible to avoid Dr This and Gina That's Essential Guide To Getting It Right. Some of my friends say the volumes available are anxious in themselves, whipping up paranoia rather than encouraging parenting skills.

It begins with whether one glass of wine is permissible during pregnancy and proceeds to Breast is Best. Deliberations about the MMR vaccination take weeks and are followed by anxious playtime monitoring, lest Child begins drawing elaborate replicas of French cathedrals after he's innoculated. The lines of cots in daycare nurseries resemble a scene from *Brave New World*, but then there was that film about the Nanny Who Took Over. Find a good school, can we get a place? Should we move house? The prices are inflated in that area but how else do you get in? The race to ensure one's child gets the best start in life has never been more fraught with concern. And all the time the gap between the haves and have-nots in our society is widening.

3. Competitiveness

I Don't Know How She Does It, Allison Pearson called her best-selling novel about a stressed-out working Mum. I Don't Know Why She Does It, more like. As if the juggling act isn't tricky enough, something is causing women with good jobs and beautiful children to feel bad if they don't have time to pack lunchboxes themselves, preferably with homegrown produce from the vegetable patch in their garden. Parenthood has become a competitive sport. Even mothers who successfully combine a career and children seem prepared to risk nervous exhaustion for the sake of one-upmanship. Those Dads that make it to Sports Day have been in training for weeks and run the Father's Race in spikes and lycra. Until recently an American glossy magazine ran a 'Working Mother of the Year' contest. It was dropped when a new editor pointed out that parenthood isn't an Olympic category. Yet.

4. Perpetual Emotion ...

> Every morning when I leave for work Rory cries and pleads with me not to go. It's heartbreaking and means that my days begin with tears – always Rory's and often mine.
>
> *Annie, 37, healthcare manager, Bristol*

> I'd been on a business trip and when I got back I asked Jasper if he loved mummy or our nanny Moira the most. I know it was wrong, but he tactfully replied that he liked us 'both the same' and Moira had to go.
>
> *Emma, 39, chartered accountant*

5. ... or Ever Decreasing Circles

Stay at Home Mum is the currently acceptable title for mothers who look after their children full-time, but it's only an updated version of the frowned-upon *'er indoors*. Practicalities limit the horizons of parents who look after their children full-time because movement is restricted to the North–South compass points of home and school. East might be Beavers and West might be a sleepover, but the people one's mixing with are all leading similar lives. Friends are not chosen so freely – parents often have to make do with whoever their children turn up with. Going out is a treat that requires advance planning; stray too far and risk being late for the babysitter.

When I look at the Friends Reunited website and see that Annabel Johnson is *still living in Purley*! with two children *at the same school we went to*! and *teaching piano*! in *what spare time I have with two children*! – I feel like I've eaten a plate of lumpy mashed potato, redolent of our classroom years.

6. Conformity

If there is a biological imprint that makes some people want babies more than others, then it's a blessing to have been born without it. For every prospective parent who claims that having children won't change their lives, ten with experience will acknowledge that they will. Announcing a pregnancy is the first rung on a ladder of convention that's of little interest to childfree people. Experts agree that children need routines, boundaries, regular food, baths, comfort and stability. Attending mother and baby groups, hosting birthday parties, watching school plays, saying 'keep your elbows off the table' and joining the PTA are but a few more of the myriad conformities that parents become inevitably embroiled in, willingly or otherwise, for a very long number of years. Not having to spend every weekday morning between 8.15 and 8.45 bumper to bumper in school-run traffic, is enough on its own to make being childfree a good option.

> I have been passionately interested in human rights since my student days and for ten years I worked in the fund-raising department of a charity that campaigns for better conditions for overseas prisoners. When our second child arrived the salary was simply not big enough to support us all so I moved to a better-paid job. It's less interesting and I have to wear a suit every day, which may sound like no big deal, except that it's just not me. I sold out when I had kids, if the truth be told.
>
> *Duncan, 37*

Political research has consistently shown that people identify more with conservative values as they grow older. 'Once you have children,' a friend adds, 'your instincts change. I used to believe in rehabilitation for criminals, now I just want them Off My Streets!'

7. Change of Self

Women change when they have babies and some of us don't want to change. It's common for mothers of young children to say they can't bear to watch disturbing news footage or films about children struggling to survive in poor countries. The thought of being too insulated doesn't feel right for some people. As parents do their best to protect their children from an often frightening and destructive world, the more privileged among them risk growing up with little idea how 'the other half lives'.

Not long ago, covering the story of a convicted rapist who'd served his prison sentence but was subsequently suspected of strangling two teenagers, I arrived with other journalists at the house of his mother. We were looking for relatives to talk to, but on the locked front door she'd already pinned a handwritten message which gave us our quote. 'I love my son Tony unconditionally to the day I die,' it read. The journalists walked down the drive, debating whether the note was best interpreted as an ultimate reflection of love conquering evil, or a frightening indictment of motherhood changing a woman, literally beyond reason.

8. Trouble and Strife

Happily single, childfree people reap the rewards of independence and freedom and account for another rising statistic in our changing demography.[1] For those in a couple, an added benefit of a childfree relationship is having the time to really share life with your partner.

As for my husband – my heart is knit to him.

Charlotte Brontë

In the UK, the average couple with children spends 78 minutes a day awake together while couples without children manage three hours a day.[2] Children are one of the main causes of arguments between parents[3] and though (I can assure) there are plenty more topics that willingly suffice, families-of-two don't get ground down with repetitive bickering about who's been ferrying the kids around most. The depressing scenario of 'staying together for the sake of the children' doesn't arise and, unless she's very unlucky, the childfree woman will never share her bed at night with a man who slips into the habit of calling her Mum. Many older parents describe an emotional distance later in life, brought about by years of focusing on the children at the expense of their own relationship. Once the kids leave home, they face each other across the empty breakfast table and think, 'who is this person?'

9. Empty Nest Syndrome

All those of years of background banter, tears and triumphs, fights about what's on TV and, suddenly, it's gone – two-odd decades of life disappearing behind a backpack or wrapped in a uni scarf: a rude awakening to your own mortality. Some say children keep you young, others that they make you old before your time.

'You'll be lonely', childfree people are warned, but we're not – we've been out there living our lives (or at least curled up on the sofa with a pot of coffee and a good book). In a cruel twist, real loneliness hits mothers who've devoted their lives to their children with little thought for themselves. It's the loneliness of rejection, when your grown-up kids visit, but you know it's out of duty; they move away or they don't invite you for Christmas. Babies are sweet-smelling bundles of hope and purpose, but they only stay for a while.

> I had my children in the 1950s – all the women in my street did the homemaker thing – nobody thought otherwise then. I was utterly absorbed by my four for 30 years. In the mid-1980s the last one left home and the nest was empty. I did have a job as a secretary when I was first married, but everything moved on and I never learned to use a computer. The thought of going back to work was laughable really – even if I'd had the confidence to try, who'd have wanted me? I was devastated when the children were gone, my life hasn't felt complete since.
>
> *Doreen, great-grandmother*

Recruitment experts say that confidence is so low among women who return to work after bringing up their children that they'll put up with anything.

10. To Infinity and Beyond

High house prices have resulted in people staying at home longer and the trend is for women to get pregnant later in life than they did in the past. The seasons of life are changing and there's not even a prospect of a break in the autumn any more because often now, grandparents are called on as primary child carers. While many enjoy the role (the Empty Nest is full again!) – many have mixed feelings.

> My daughter and son-in-law both work full-time and have a house with a big mortgage. They commute into London and don't get home until seven, so Ray (my husband) and I have the children after school most days and all through the holidays. We don't think it's right to let them watch too much television, so we help them with their homework or play a board game. We don't mind, but it's tiring and it's not what we expected. My own mum used to say that when Ruth (my daughter) was small, she had the best of both worlds because she could enjoy her, then give her back to me.
>
> Ray used to say we'd be living in Majorca and going on cruises when we retired, but there's none of that.
>
> *Effie, 60, Buckinghamshire*

'We are not a childcare service!' a frustrated grandparent wrote to Age Concern, which cites childcare responsibilities as a major reason for the over fifties leaving employment before they want to. The more older people leave the work force, the more the fashion for youth culture is perpetuated in commerce to the detriment of wiser folk. One in four grandparents – often skilled and relatively young themselves – is now routinely bringing up children.[4] It must make the charity's campaign against ageism even harder than it is already.

Being childfree? It's the best kept secret!

Lionel Shriver
writer
b 1957

We Need to Talk About Kevin (Serpent's Tail)

In We Need to Talk About Kevin, *Lionel Shriver weaves her own doubts and fears about motherhood into a gripping plot. It's the story of a family's personal tragedy – set in America where everything works, nobody starves and anything can be bought except a sense of purpose. Shriver's main character Eva Khatchadourian never wanted children, but was coerced into it by her husband. They produce Kevin, who grows into a difficult child and a disaffected teenager. Shortly before his 16th birthday, he murders seven of his classmates in an all too realistic high school massacre of the kind we've seen on the TV news.*

I'd always been pretty sure I didn't want children, but getting into my forties I felt I needed to properly investigate my reasons and ensure I wasn't making a wrong decision. So my own thoughts inspired the book and in turn it was cathartic. I came out knowing my instinct was right and I've remained childless.

ND: It's a heavy subject matter?

Yes, but such awful things do happen, and the risk of having my own baby that was something like Kevin was one I considered. There is no guarantee your children will turn out like the Waltons. Most families are dysfunctional in a manageable way, some are dysfunctional to the point of misery and destruction. I concluded that my own life is all the things I want it to be, and wouldn't be enhanced by a baby.

ND: What was your personal biggest fear about having children?

That I would have a child with awful consequences and regrets for the both of us. You can ruin kids in plenty of ways. They don't have to become killers, that was an extreme for the plot. But I do believe there are thousands of women out there whose children have not turned out as they'd hoped and are unhappy or in trouble in some way. The mothers feel responsible but of course they can't say so. I wouldn't expect them to because expression could add to the hurt all round, but it must be lonely keeping it to themselves.

ND: So when the character Eva is considering whether to try for a baby, how much of you is coming through?

All of the character is me at this stage.

> *After all, now that children don't till your fields or take you in when you're incontinent, there is no sensible reason to have them, and it's amazing that with the advent of effective contraception, anyone chooses to reproduce at all.*

ND: And when Eva becomes pregnant, how did you guess how she'd feel?

I just used my gut instinct. I imagined being told I was expecting a baby and wrote the dialogue that expressed my feelings:

> *'It's positive,' [the doctor] said crisply. 'Are you alright, you've turned white?'*
>
> *I did feel strangely cold.*
>
> *'Eva, this should be good news.' She said this severely, with reproach. I got the impression that if I wasn't going to be happy about it, she would take my baby and give it to somebody who'd got their mind right –*

who would hop up and down like a game show contestant who'd won the car.

ND: Tell me a little more about your own reasons for not wanting children.

They are mainly based on observations of my own mother. Motherhood to me seems a formula for being taken less seriously. I grew up in Atlanta, Georgia, in a hierarchical family structure. It was very important that my dad earned the most money and was head of the household. Mum went along with it passively and acted as though it was fine that way, lavishing him with praise. She did everything for him – it was way beyond healthy support – but typical of her peers at that time. I remember thinking this was a stupid way to be. She never stood her ground, just accepted everything that came her way, and Dad got the credit for everything because of course homemakers never get any praise.

When I was 15, Mum was offered a job and there was huge turmoil because the salary was bigger than my father's. Dad taught in the Divinity School at the local university and Mum was given a post aligned to the Church. Dad was very nervous about it all and his attitude certainly didn't inspire the pride in her which was due. I hated the way she deferred to him, was grateful to him for allowing her the opportunity of going out to work and was self-deprecating to a fault to avoid any possibility of upstaging him.

ND: So your mum took up the job?

Yes and she went from strength to strength. They're still together and still run things much the same way, but going out to work definitely gave Mum an extra dimension.

ND: Does she ever talk to you about motherhood?

In my late thirties I met a guy I was serious about and we spoke about how he was 'the one' and the opportunities we might have in life together. She said 'if you

value your relationship, don't have children'. The way she emphasised how a relationship between a couple changes made a great impression on me.

After Kevin is sent to prison, Eva writes letters to her estranged husband, reflecting on their lives together as a family as she tries to find meaning for what happened. She explains how she felt her husband treated her when she was pregnant:

Your proprietary attitude was grating. If I ever cut it close crossing the street you weren't concerned for my personal safety but were outraged at my irresponsibility. These 'risks' I took – and I regarded as going about my regular life – seemed in your mind to exhibit a cavalier attitude toward one of your personal belongings. Every time I walked out the door I swear you glowered a little, as if I was bearing away one of your prized possessions without asking.

ND: What is your father like?

Mum got more out of being around us children than Dad did when we were small. I felt he found us annoying and he often talked about how he longed for the day we could have adult conversations together. I identify much more with my father than my mother. He seemed to have the better deal. Children don't interest me until they're about ten. I don't like talking down to young kids because it seems patronising, but if I talk normally they don't understand so I'm not that comfortable with them. Small children are tyrannically boring. I would rather shoot myself than sit on the floor and play with their bricks and I think my dad felt the same.

ND: How do you enjoy your life?

I do whatever I want and have so much liberty. I try not to take it for granted because my independence is hard won. But most people are setting an alarm for 6.30, shoving down breakfast, getting a family out the door, sitting in a jam. I don't have that. The way the modern world is it's amazing anyone has children. Both partners work and childcare costs a fortune. Family life doesn't work, economically, logistically or emotionally. I think often people must have children to provide a sense of meaning and fulfil that existential hunger. Kids certainly fill up a schedule, but they complicate things beyond belief.

ND: People say childfree women will have regrets, does that bother you?

Not now that I've so thoroughly examined my thoughts and feelings on the matter. Writing them in We Need to Talk About Kevin really clarified everything. I never bought into the theory that things are different when it's your own child and writing in the character of Eva was like writing about my own child. I came through knowing it wasn't for me.

> ***What possessed us? We were so happy! Why, then, did we take the stake of all we had and place it all on this outrageous gamble of having a child?***

II

Childfree and Loving It! Positive Stories of Childfree People

In the course of my research I made two small website postings – one on a childfree network and another on a parents network. They resulted in a steady influx of mail. Childfree people seemed delighted that their lifestyles were to be written about in a positive way and filled in the questionnaires I sent them with considerable detail. Most made a point of saying that it was high time the validity of being a non-parent became accepted in mainstream media, rather than restricted to internet groups. The response from parents was slow to begin with, but when I amended my initial request for contributors and made clear that identities would be concealed, things picked up considerably. For a few months, rarely a day went by without a note from a parent appearing in my inbox. I would have loved to include everyone, but even the stories of those who didn't make it into print found their way into my subconscious and so, onto the page.

Given the response, it seemed fitting to include as many upbeat testimonies to being childfree as was possible. These are just some of the people who are *childfree and loving it!*

I knew from the age of about seven that I never wanted children, I didn't feel as though I had to make a choice. My aunt Hazel was a great role model. She had a beautiful flat in London, drove a Mini and owned two dogs. When I was small it seemed she had the ideal life. She used to take me to the theatre and out to tea and buy me nice presents. I only went to stay once a year or so when I was growing up, but those visits had a big influence on me. I think my mum may have pointed out (in exasperation) the connection between Aunt Hazel's lifestyle and her not having children. I used to go home and ask why we didn't live like Aunt Hazel!

ND: What are the best things about your choice?

FREEDOM! I have freedom to keep working which means the excitement of regularly shopping in New York or San Francisco; freedom to wake up naturally most mornings; freedom to spend my money on myself or on joint projects with my husband; freedom to spend the day reading a book or at a spa or beauty salon; freedom to please myself without carrying out obligations to feed, clothe, wash, teach and play with a small child; freedom from a stroppy toddler or teenager's mood swings; freedom from mother-and-toddler groups; freedom to let my mind wander rather than tying it to a child's routines; freedom of my own body unchanged by pregnancy and childbirth; freedom of equality with my husband; freedom to pursue any goals I care to imagine.

ND: How do people react to you choosing not to have children?

My mother and grandmother support my choice and I have an aunt and uncle who chose not to have children so I have never felt any pressure. My oldest friend has three children and she respects my choice (as I respect hers).

The only negative reactions I've experienced have come from strangers or colleagues. I've been called selfish, but their opinions bounce away as they don't know anything about my life. I can only assume they feel jealous because it didn't occur to them that they had a choice. If I'm criticised I say that both parents and non-parents are equally selfish because we all follow our desires.

ND: Why do you think people have children?

I honestly feel that people have children to feel possession of another human being.

To be truly unselfish we would adopt the millions of unwanted children that already exist and not create more. The names people give their children tell me a lot about their reasons for having them. They are often so full of aspiration — a class above the parents. It is all about recreating a better version of yourself using someone else.

My answer is why not create a better version of yourself, using yourself? I would rather fulfil my own potential than inflict my ambitions on some other poor sap!

The reality for me is that my parent friends will regularly comment, albeit jokingly, about how lucky I am not to have kids for some reason or other, whereas I have never felt anything but relief that I am not in their position.

ND: Are you concerned you'll regret your decision?

Absolutely not. As I get older I increasingly appreciate the benefits of my situation.

ND: Any other comments?
The area I feel most strongly about is that becoming a parent is never questioned or discussed – it is considered naturally to be the most fulfilling, correct decision for everybody – as though one size fits all, like buying a scarf in Gap.

As I was writing all this down, I wondered why I was writing so much. I realised it was due to relief, because my opinions are distasteful to the common view and I always censor them. To be honest I wouldn't care if I never saw my friends' children again but I could never express that to them.

My choice to be childfree threatens people sometimes because it acknowledges a dark and hidden truth that our society cannot tolerate; namely that being a parent is not a nirvana for everybody. But saying these things – it's like confessing a dark secret.

Joanna Knight, 37, airline cabin crew, Cheshire, UK

My partner Adella and I have been together for six years. We met through a dating agency! I wanted to meet a woman who felt the same way about life as I did and we had a strong bond from the start. Both of us had written on our application forms that we didn't want children. I always wanted to share life with someone I love on an equal footing. I'm not sure that children make that very easy because caring for them necessitates a demarcation of roles. I can't pretend I would have the interest in looking after a child that many women seem to find naturally, and I think women get a raw deal when it comes to doing most of the child orientated stuff.

The women I went out with in my thirties wanted to get married and have a baby. It seemed so predictable in this day and age. It didn't seem fair to go along with the idea that it might happen with me, because women have this time pressure. I ended a few relationships because of it and one in particular was a woman I loved very much. But I knew the relationship would change if I compromised so I kind of wrenched myself away. Her friends gave me a really hard time about it. I was hurt by that because I was only trying to be fair to both of us.

It has never occurred to me that children might enhance my life. For one thing all I see is evidence to the contrary. The parents I know are tense, time starved and don't seem to enjoy their relationship with each other in the way Adella and I do. That was always the most important thing to me.

My two sisters don't want kids for much the same reasons as me. My own parents say they never wanted children, but in their day choice didn't really come into it. Mum and Dad were competent parents but their lives didn't revolve around us. As we grew up we developed our own interests and took our own paths. We didn't rely on them for stimulation or entertainment and perhaps that's influenced our decisions.

Adella and I lead a calm and peaceful existence which suits us. We try to live with integrity. Occasionally on a Friday night we have thought 'Let's go to Paris on the Eurostar tomorrow!' and we have done. It's lovely. We are the most important people in each other's lives, we share everything and I wouldn't have it any other way.

James, 45, archivist, London

When I was in my early twenties I always assumed I would have children, just not yet. The assumption of a future with children was common among others my age, along with the ultra-casual assumptions that we actually were able to have them and that we would do so with our life partners at the time of our choosing. By the time I was about 28 I realised that there was an alternative positive choice that

I wanted to make. My contemporaries – men and women – were clearly experiencing a near-primeval need to reproduce, whether or not they were in a position to go ahead. This was an instinct which I simply didn't feel. If a friend had a baby it was great. I quite liked holding the baby out of curiosity and I quite liked getting a close-up view. But I didn't find babies or children fascinating and adorable in the way that so many other people seemed to. Never at any time did I feel the tiniest need to have one myself.

My life is about all the things that are in it, not the things that are not in it. Being childfree comes naturally to me just as parenting does to others, but it must be relevant that I always enjoyed living on my own during my twenties. One of the aspects I most value about my relationship with my partner is that he is away quite a lot, so it seems to me the best of all worlds. If I have to think about it, I know I am an insanely tidy person and would loathe the mess that children bring. I don't like the noise they make, and of course they cost a lot. The implied self-sacrifice of parenthood can be nauseating.

My mother has always assumed that my desire not to have children is something I will recover from. I have a very complicated relationship with my mother, but I am certain that has nothing to do with my choice because I simply don't feel any instinctive urge to have children. I am certainly relieved that I will not be reproducing my own relationship with my mother in any child of my own. I have also chosen to remain unmarried, another illness from which she awaits my recovery.

Alison, 40, London

My home as a child was fantastic! I had a glorious childhood. I grew up in rural north Louisiana where there were literally no other children in my neighbourhood. I was accustomed very early on to having quiet, mature, stable adults around me. I was a huge tomboy. I loved climbing trees and riding horses. I wasn't pushed into any gender roles, my parents just made sure that I was happy and that I learned to be kind to myself and others and they made sure that I did well in school. I liked seeing my peers at school, but I liked even more coming home to a quiet house. Mom and Dad never mentioned anything about 'when you grow up and have kids' – probably because they saw I hated dolls and never liked being around babies. The best gift they gave me was that I was simply allowed to grow up and be myself and they loved me just as I was. That makes me so happy even today!

ND: What are your main reasons for choosing a childfree lifestyle?

As a child, whenever I saw a pregnant woman I always thought it was weird. I always felt my body is mine and I want nothing invading it. I would hate the horrors of childbirth and being treated like an intellectual infant by obstetricians and midwives. Having children would be a way of being 'tamed' that makes me bristle. Nobody tames me. Nobody confines me. Nobody sets limits on my freedom or prescribes my life path for me.

I knew from childhood I wanted a very loving, peer marriage with nothing to come between me and my partner, especially children. All those so-called jokes about not enough sex and not enough money really aren't jokes. I saw when I was very young that living like men do is a path of independence, freedom and success, but living like a traditional woman is a path of dependence, confinement and economic deprivation. I refuse to be traditional. I am a human being first, Katie second and female last.

ND: Do you have philosophical reasons for not having children as well as lifestyle reasons?
Giving birth is not only about giving life. A child will usually outlive its parent, but the child will die. It's just that the parent isn't there to bear witness. I will never give life, so I will never be responsible for someone's death. As much as life may be wonderful, it can also be full of suffering.
ND: What do you like most about your life?
I value peace, serenity and harmony in my relationships. Having a child wouldn't allow that. A child's job is to differentiate from its parents and although that's normal, it's not fun or peaceful or without angst or strife. I can't bear screaming, I can't stand arguments and I get extremely stressed when someone is defiant, lying, etc. Children are going to act these things out as part of their growth process, but I have my own growth to attend to.

Teaching is my calling and vocation. I believe to the marrow of my bones in education and I really like working with teens. I'm just happy not to have to take them home.
ND: Describe your life now.
My husband and I make enough money to be very comfortable. I was married before to a much older guy (also childfree) but we didn't have much in common. Now I have found my soulmate. We have a large house with lots of room for us, our books and our cats. I am so glad I kept my eyes wide open as a kid. I analysed everything and saw the reality of having children rather than just the rosy picture that everyone paints. I have the life I've chosen and it's wonderful.
ND: How do people react to you?
My family has always reacted positively to me but we are a bunch of rugged individualists. My family is not into stereotyping, rigid gender roles, impressing other people or caring what they think.

Outside my family, I've gotten the line that I should have children but there seemed to be a nasty undercurrent of eugenics. I am white, educated, middle class and people have implied that 'we need more of your type'. It appals me. There are those who say, 'You'll change your mind,' when I state my well-thought-out choice and there are those who are threatened by women who are humans first and not just walking wombs. People have asked me, 'What if your mother had said she didn't want children?' and I've replied, 'Then you'd be standing here talking to yourself.' You cannot force someone into a pre-made mould.

I have seen women asked 'How many children do you have?' which is damn tactless. The non-assuming phrasing is, 'Do you have any children?' When someone says no, I wish, I WISH, people would just move on to another topic of conversation! I hate when people don't accept my answer of 'I just don't want to.' That's what it boils down to anyway.

ND: Any other comments?

It's no longer necessary to have children to be a part of the greater community. What is necessary is to give back to the community of one's time, talents and resources.

We have a right to make the very best of ourselves with the talents we have.

Having children in the future may be no more than an expensive hobby.

Katie Andrews, 35, teacher, Los Angeles, California

I think a couple should only have children if both of them really desire it and neither my wife nor I do. I want to lead my own life (not my kid's life), and I don't feel the need to have children. Other reasons, like social acceptance, the perpetuation of the family line or insurance for old age may make other people decide to have children, but not me.

In Belgium, where I come from, it's often implied that people who choose not to have children are selfish. I rather think it is the other way round, as people don't have children for the children's sake but for their own. Parents expect gratitude from their children because they 'gave them life' but I don't see why this should be the case. Nobody asks to be born and parents should not expect anything in return. It's really quite hypocritical to say CF people are selfish.

I am always hearing 'you've got it easy, you don't have kids', which is annoying because anyone could have made the same choice as me. My mother was for a long time giving oblique hints about grandchildren, but now she seems to accept that we won't have kids. Apart from that, I don't get many reactions on the topic, it seems not to be an issue.

People think having kids makes them more important and allows them all kinds of liberties. A typical example is parents with a huge pram with a tiny baby (and loads of shopping) who want to get on the bus and take up a large amount of space. They could just as well have a smaller pram and fold it, or why not carry their baby in a sling like one of my friends used to do? Baby likes it and it takes up no space at all. Also, a lot of people use their kids to justify the over-frequent use of their car.

When I look at friends and family, those with nice kids don't take them so seriously (or themselves), mostly because they have a job of their own too.

For a man in Belgium, having a wife and kids is a prerequisite for a successful management career. This must be something subconscious, but it is a fact. It does not apply to technical positions where having no kids is an advantage because dads with young kids are always tired, so not very efficient in their jobs. For women, having no children is an advantage for a professional career.

All societies and cultures promote and encourage having kids. As a consequence, there is a strong social pressure to have them, just to conform. Most governments give support to people with children. Essentially, it means people without children pay for other people to have children. I think that is not quite fair. In my opinion, governments should not encourage people to have kids while at the same time putting a stop on immigration. The planet is already overpopulated – we could share around more.

Very few people will disagree with the idea that mankind must persist at all cost. Personally, I would not care. After the last human has gone, who will be there to regret it?

Maarten, 36, academic, Belgium

Derek and I had both been in previous, unhappy marriages when we met and we were so pleased to have found each other that we didn't want to change anything. We were in our late thirties then. Most of our friends had had kiddies in their twenties and we were so much older it seemed like we'd already missed the boat. There was still time but we wanted time just for us too. We talked about it a lot, just Derek and me, and eventually we decided we wouldn't have children. It was the 1970s and both our families were quite rude after we got married and the months went by and I didn't get pregnant. They kept telling us how we were missing out on so much. In the end we let them think I was infertile and they treated us with pity, as though we must be devastated that we couldn't have the whole little postcard family.

Life would have been different if we had had children, I know that. I'll never know if it would have been better or worse. I'm perfectly happy as I am but would I have been happier? That's something I'll never know.

June, 68, Melbourne, Australia

I have no interest whatsoever in children, mine or anyone else's. I've never really made a choice – having children is something I have never given any thought to. I love having few responsibilities and being to do what I like when I like. I don't just mean lying in bed at weekends (though that's nice too!) but a couple of years ago I felt I needed a complete change, so I sold my flat and packed in the job I'd had for ten years. I did temporary work and rented somewhere to live, which wouldn't have been possible with children to think about. I work full-time as well as co-running a small business and I enjoy going out and socialising. I wouldn't be able to do this (or have the money for it) if I had children and I wouldn't like the constant demands that they make. I look at friends who are parents and their lives are not their own and won't be for a long time yet. I couldn't stand living like that. When I tell people I don't want kids I am usually met with surprise and the hackneyed phrase 'you'll feel different when they're your own'. I told someone once how ridiculous this sounded – that if I'd said I didn't like dogs, for instance, no one would say to me 'you'll feel different when you get your own puppy!' That was just met with a puzzled expression.

I don't mind children but the parents annoy me and I think society is raising a generation of extremely spoiled and self-centred people. I certainly don't want to be a part of that.

I think most people think I am hard or selfish or both, but actually I'm neither. I care about a lot of things – animals, the environment, my friends and family. I've recently finished a temporary job answering calls on a health and social care helpline. I did it for 18 months and found helping people with their problems very rewarding.

Alex, 41, civil servant, London

I am Dutch and before I migrated to Australia a few years back I ran a childfree website in the Netherlands and I wanted to do something similar here, but on a bigger scale, so I set up the World Childfree Association (WCA). We aim to unify childfree people around the world. At first, WCA was only available in English and Dutch, but volunteer translators started to offer their services and we now have 18 languages waiting to be uploaded. We organise lots of social events through the website and are asked to do interviews on the subject of being childfree almost on a weekly basis by the media of different countries (Norway, Turkey, Brazil, the US, and of course the Netherlands and Australia so far). We have an online magazine written by the childfree for the childfree and have been debating with gynaecologists about why it is so difficult for women to organise a sterilisation if they don't want children.

ND: What is your background?

I migrated to Australia because I got tired of the Netherlands. I'm a person who is always looking for new challenges. I don't want my life to be the same for the next 30 (or longer) years, living in the same house, the same suburb, sitting in the same job, doing the same things every day. I like changes and making decisions that have a major impact on my life. My husband and I want to live on a boat in the future, where our living environment will change every day. Life at sea will be full of challenges. There are also some more dull reasons why I left the Netherlands: I couldn't stand the weather, always grey and grumpy, which made me feel depressed.

ND: What are your main reasons for choosing a childfree lifestyle?

I've simply never felt the urge to become a mother and as young as I can remember I've always known that I never wanted to have kids. I am concerned about world population and crime. If I had a daughter I would always fear for her safety. You could say that I love my unborn kids too much to bring them into a world like this. Life is a struggle to me.

Most people seem to be so different from myself. Nobody seems to have dreams, ambitions or drive anymore. They go to work every day to earn their daily bread and they are happy with that, but I want so much more from life. When I die I want to be able to look myself in the eyes and say: 'You have done everything you wanted to do in this life. You can now rest peacefully.' Because I'm so driven, I often get into conflicts with other people, because I expect too much from them – I expect the same from them as I expect from myself. Every day has only so many hours, of which the biggest part is spent either working or sleeping. I wish I had more time to do the things that I want to do.

ND: How do people react to you?

It gets better the older I get. My mother only recently (a couple of years ago) started to realise that I meant what I said about not having children when I told her I had a tubal ligation when I was 22, my hubby had a vasectomy at 30 and I was maintaining a childfree website. She is still a bit hostile towards my choice. She says she's accepted it, but at the same time she gives me all those prejudices, just like all the other people with children do. She thinks for example, that my career was the logical alternative to kids, without realising that I actually hate working. I work as hard as I do to be able to stop working as soon as possible, so that I can start enjoying life.

In the past some Christian colleagues were disgusted by the fact that I didn't want children. They told me that 'I had insulted all women around the world', that 'God had meant women to have children' and that 'women were built to suffer the pain of giving birth.' It's crap. But these days I've got pretty cool colleagues who I've shown my website and they actually agree with me. My boss is even proud to be managing 'a little celebrity' (because of my media interviews all the time).

ND: What do you think it's like being a child in today's world?

I'm very worried for the children that are born today, what life they will have in the future in terms of what the planet has to offer them. Here in Australia we have been living under strict water restrictions for quite a while now and there is even talk of rationing the water. That makes you really wonder how much water will be left for today's children. Water is one of our basic needs for survival, so if that becomes scarce, you can imagine what happens next: war.

ND: Do you feel discriminated against for being childfree?

Oh yes, very much. For example, a friend wanted to make a trip with the Thalys (the train that runs from Amsterdam to Marseille). As a single adult, she would pay €150. However, if she were a mum with a child, she would only pay €45! The child travels for free and the mum pays for only a third of what a person without a child would pay.

ND: Does anyone get it right when it comes to raising children?

I can only speak of my own experience, but Asian children on outings with their parents seem well behaved, and a friend tells me Greek families, while adoring their kids, ensure they are well behaved. In Australia and the Netherlands children are treated like little gods. They are indulged and spoiled and often not corrected in their bad behaviour because 'they are only children', which I find infuriating. For some reason, parents fail to see that if you don't correct your children now, later on they will not be able to tell the difference between right and wrong.

ND: Any other comments?

Other things that I find annoying is that parents, especially mothers, don't seem to be able to talk about anything but their children. I dislike the way children are valued differently by the media. A disaster is less of a disaster if there aren't any children involved, and more of a disaster if white middle-class children are involved.

Marije Feddema, 28, business analyst and founder of the World Childfree Association, Sydney, Australia

Beware! Parents have a code of secrecy and won't tell you the downsides until it's too late. I am the oldest of six children. When I was younger I always had to look after my younger brothers or help them read or tidy up after them. I couldn't say for definite it's what put me off but I think it was a definite start along the no children road.

I don't feel the need to prove myself by having children – I'm a worthwhile person in my own right. I also like my freedom. I can cook whatever I want, get a takeaway if I don't feel like cooking and go to the cinema on a Sunday morning when it's cheap and empty. I feel tied down enough by my cats and I can leave them at home on their own all day.

Most of my friends have children. It's not an issue, I fit around them, but it would be nice if they got a babysitter and made more of an effort sometimes. I've been married five years. Both my mum and my husband's family have got used to the fact that we're not planning on children. My mother-in-law says 'I've got two grandchildren, so I'm happy with them'.

While I have made a positive choice not to have children, it is incredibly hard not to feel like there is something wrong with me as a woman. Everywhere I look there are images of famous people with their family – oh and there's another glamorous mum who's lost all her baby weight, blah, blah, blah. Usually if a woman has chosen not to have children she is portrayed as a batty old lady who lives with her cats. I feel immense pressure from friends who say things like 'Who will look after you when you're older?' What a stupid reason to have children. Imagine how upset the kids might feel if they overheard the reason they've been brought into the world. Friends also say, 'You'll have a family one day,' 'Soon you'll want kids,' and 'You don't know what you're missing.' I'm terrified that I'll wake up one morning and want to have children. Imagine the I-told-you-so's if that happens!

Lucy, 30, training centre manager, Bristol, UK

I never wanted children. I grew up fascinated by film and throughout my teens watched old black and white movies over and over. Joan Crawford and Katharine Hepburn were my favourites. Katharine Hepburn was outspoken about not wanting children which was bold and pioneering for her day. She said she was ambitious and always knew that she would not have children because she wanted total freedom. The things she cared about most were Spencer Tracy, her privacy and her career, in roughly that order. The stars of the films I watched were feisty women – they weren't domesticated even back in the 30s and 40s. It seemed to me that the characters without children always had a better time. You saw them in car chases and solving mysteries. The heroines shared a camaraderie that appealed to me. In the movies of the 1950s, women characters stopped drinking and started making the dinner. Doris Day was popular. The excitement was lost and the gingham and apple pie thing didn't inspire me in the same way. Of course they were relying on gin and valium to keep up the image anyway.

Louise, 38, actress, London

I was Saatchi and Saatchi's creative director in Hong Kong for 12 years earning a six figure salary, then I thought, 'Bugger it. Life's too short for all this stress.' I felt like a cloud had lifted. I'd gone into advertising because it was supposed to be a creative environment, but it was very corporate and controlled. You can't control creativity. I stayed abroad for a while and tried to live like a hippie, but I couldn't get away from the ex-pat crowd. I'd always had this notion of being a stand-up comic, I don't know where it came from. When I came back to London I went to a comedy workshop and liked it. I began to get work in local pubs and bars. I don't make a living from it so I do other odd jobs, but I'm free. You can have money and no time or time and no money, and I definitely prefer the second way. It's terrifying standing in front of an audience, I practise on my friends first. Once I was heckled so badly I went home and cried. I didn't go back on stage for weeks.

I knew I would never have kids. I didn't want them. In my era at school, the message was that you should go to university so that you could keep up with your husband intellectually (when you met him, that is). I'm the only person from my year who has never been married. I didn't meet Mr Darcy so it was better to be by myself. Women I know in their late thirties often get married to men they wouldn't have looked at a few years earlier. Society is still bound up in a medieval procedure; 'When will I meet Mr Right?' 'I'd better meet him soon'. Women are expected to be mothers before they can become individuals. Educated, intelligent women are reduced to talking about their children.

I'm never lonely, I like my own time and have lots of friends. When women become mothers they jettison their friends, except the ones they can talk to about school uniforms and nannies. Some of their husbands are extremely arrogant in how they view a single woman. It's all so ... traditional. They assume you're desperate and have even made passes at me!

I wanted to be an adult even when I was a child. I find children boring and repetitive. I do mix with both adults and children and it's important to accept change, but there's a limit to how long I'll sit with a child talking about poo-poo. A four-year-old talks more drivel than the tabloids and I don't read them, but you can't be objective because people's children are an extension of themselves. Their parents find them fascinating and assume you do too. I have a niece and a nephew who are great. I tell them they're lucky to have a spinster aunt and if they're mean to me they'll get no inheritance. I had the menopause in my early forties and I thought, 'Thank God, what a relief.'

Aggie Elsden, 54, comedian, London

I come from a large, close family and because I'm the type of person who likes the idea of family and tradition and quite enjoys the company of children, I thought that I'd want children eventually. But my inner voice kept telling me that parenting was not a good choice for me. It was difficult to give up the dutiful feeling that I should parent at least one kid at some point in my life. But as time passed, the reasons against having children grew and thankfully I was sharp enough to avoid making a mistake that would've negatively affected the rest of my life.

ND: What do you like most about your life?

Knowing that I can pursue my own personal happiness free from the responsibilities of parenting, and that I have not contributed to this planet's overpopulation problem.

ND: How do people react to you?

This varies depending on the experience and mindset of the people I meet. People who wrap a lot of their identity into being parents find it difficult to understand how someone could feel fulfilled without being a parent. Parents who have a realistic view of the parenting experience are more likely to appreciate why someone might want to avoid going there. People who know my personality and temperament acknowledge that I would not be well suited to parenting and respect me for honouring what's best for me. My parents are bewildered by my decision and are relieved that my other siblings gave them grandchildren.

ND: Many parents say they need to leave a footprint on the world. Do you not?

No, I feel the opposite. The human desire to transcend death by leaving descendants behind is common, but since parents can't be sure that their children will be people they'd be proud of, it's risky to find comfort in assuming they'll be positive extensions of their lives. If one wants to leave a lasting impact on humanity, why not devote time and energy into pursuits that one has more control over? Generating or promoting influential ideas, creating or supporting inspiring works in the arts, forming or being part of organisations that enhance society, etc.

ND: What do you think it's like being a child in today's world?

The world today is more complex, overwhelming and disturbing than it's ever been. However, many are insulated from this by over-protective or oblivious parents. They are not encouraged to develop the ability to see the world as it really is and find their own positive place within it.

Unfortunately, it appears that the majority of parents give more importance to fulfilling their desire to procreate than to considering what the needs and tribulations of their children could potentially be once they arrive on the planet.

ND: Do you feel society is indulgent to children?

As a music teacher for 18 years, I have noticed a deterioration in most children's ability to sit still, apply themselves, commit to lessons and practice and follow directions from authority figures. I don't think parents realise it is their job to set boundaries and guide their children, not to spoil them by showering them with most of their wants.

ND: Do you have pets?

Dogs (particularly puppies) have always triggered a strong, irrational nurturing response in me! As soon as I had my own house I immediately got a couple of dogs. Throw in a husband, a job where I work with children, nieces and a nephew, friends (some with children, some without) and ironically my 'childfree' life has considerable contact with children and many opportunities to fulfil any nurturing tendencies. So, it is possible to be childfree and still have positive involvement with children, while avoiding the strains and responsibilities of parenting. If more people realised this, the world would be a better place, with fewer people who were more interconnected.

ND: Any other comments?

I'm glad that the childfree subject is being addressed more frequently in academe, popular media, contemporary literature and everyday life. Childfree-ness has never been strongly highlighted in biography, but rather considered an interesting aside. I'm planning to do some research in my local community to create material for high school text books and health agencies to increase the visibility of being childfree as a valid lifestyle choice. At present the childfree comprise a marginalised group of adults whose ideas and experiences need to be heard and understood. Thanks for your work in this regard.

Theresa Torgunrud, 37, music teacher, Saskatchewan, Canada

I have never wanted children. I don't really like them. When I was 32 I had an abortion. My doctor was horrified I was so upfront about it. He asked if I wanted counselling, which I didn't. I wasn't troubled in the slightest but the reactions of other people were a pain in the neck. Even friends who were well aware of my intention not to have children said consolingly, 'When you meet the right man, you'll want to have a baby.' By the time I'd seen two doctors (as required by law) and my appointment was booked, I began to feel worn down by the over-reactions of the medical staff who were supposed to be supporting me. They made it into such a big issue – warning me of future emotional problems, the sense of loss and suffering I'd feel. Some made me feel callous for knowing my own mind, and others went on so much that sometimes I did worry I was demented or odd. I was not. I know termination is traumatic for many women, but it's not for all of us. Afterwards the hospital staff wouldn't let me get the bus home and I had to spend 30 quid on a taxi. My decision has never troubled me.

I don't believe in pregnancy as a poignant meeting of souls that results in the miraculous creation of new life. It's nice to think that, if it's planned and you're in love, but so often it's a burst condom or a grope too far. How can people apply one description to their own circumstances and another to a teenage mum on a council estate?

I met my partner Clive four years ago and we immediately felt right for each other, but it soon became apparent that our attitudes towards being parents were very different. He has three children from a previous marriage and his life has always been bound up with kids. Early on, in those heady first weeks of romance, I was amazed when Clive told me he'd love to have a baby together. He was equally shocked by my response. In his mind a baby is the mark of your love for someone and he thought his suggestion was the ultimate compliment; you meet someone, you fall in love, you have a baby together. I think it's an assumption he'd picked up along the way, but the poor guy hadn't bargained on me! We've moved on from that conversation and he appreciates the advantages of our lifestyle now. For the first time in his life he's been on holiday with just me – no parents, no kids of his own. It's like a light bulb has lit up in his head and he relishes the freedom. He told me he was knocked sideways when we spent a romantic week on holiday in the Gambia recently, just the two of us. 'I've woken up to how good the absence of children can be for a relationship,' was one of his remarks.

I would say I'm different to other people in subtle ways. I'll happily walk into a bar on my own and spend the evening there. I'd rather savour a film by myself than go with friends who might detract from my enjoyment by not liking it. I've never identified with a group, and though I love being in a relationship I don't care whether we get married.

Sarah, 39, London

When I was younger I presumed that I would have children at some point, I never really questioned it or thought about it.

Throughout my twenties I was busy studying and travelling and I went to university for four years with a year teaching and studying in Mexico. It seemed that I was enjoying my youth and independence before I settled down and had a family. But in the last five years I began to give the reality of having children serious thought. One by one my friends have had children. I'm godmother to one little girl who's a sweet little thing, but I've never felt broody myself and I've made a decision that I'd rather just get on with life. Once that decision was made, I felt rather liberated.

ND: What do you like most about your life?

Independence, freedom, space in my life to make choices and time for myself. If I want to spend a complete Sunday lying on the sofa watching old movies and eating popcorn I can and I do. Or I can spend all day planning my classes for the week (I'm a language teacher) or sitting in a bar with friends, playing cards, or walking on the beach with my dogs.

I help out at the local vet clinic and at the animal shelter in my village.

I've been called selfish for wanting to spend my life doing what I want, but I think it would be more selfish to have a child I didn't really want, regretting it and resenting it. Whenever I'm in the company of my friends with children I invariably think at some point or other, 'Thank God that's not me!'

ND: How do people react to you?

In a way I'm used to people thinking I'm a bit odd. I'm single and acquaintances presume I have no children because I have no husband, which is nonsense. My friends feel sorry for me because they think I'm missing out on this great motherhood experience. They gently remind me that time is passing — which I'm supposed to take as a kind gesture on their part. Pretty much everyone takes my decision rather negatively. I'm always being told I'll feel different when I meet the right man and some people have even presumed I'm a lesbian. The vast majority definitely see my childfree state as temporary and they expect me to see the light at some point.

It's impossible trying to air an opinion on the subject of children when you're a person without children. People just say 'well what do you know about it?' — although they are quick to criticise my way of life. I resent that. I've never met George Bush but I can discuss his politics!

ND: Many parents say they need to leave a footprint on the world. Do you not?

No, but you're right — most people do have a fantasy about producing a little replica of themselves that will go on living, moulded as they choose, when they're gone. I think many feel disappointed, betrayed even, when said child develops into something quite different to its parents, with differing opinions, morals and lifestyle choices.

ND: What do you think it is like being a child in today's world?

Stressful and dangerous. A lot of children are shunted from pillar to post to fit in with their parents' work which can't be good for the child but also causes feelings of guilt in the parents. Consequently the parent doesn't like to discipline or say 'no' to the child which just makes the child unbearable. People have fewer children than in the past so they pour all their resources into the one or two they have. I see children who are so pampered and protected that they cannot cope with not getting their own way. I wonder how these children will gain the skills they need for dealing with life as adults.

ND: Do you feel society is indulgent to children?
Much more so than in the past, but it's not possible to generalise because so many children live deprived lives. My home is in Spain and here children are viewed with humour and affection whatever they do. People don't care if a child crawls under their table when they're having dinner. Once, a child of about six was running around a restaurant and knocked over a bottle of wine my friends and I were drinking. It smashed on the floor. The view was that the child had frightened himself and everyone rallied around him. There was no question that his parents would replace our wine, which I would have done in reverse. If you had the audacity to ask parents to keep their children quiet, you would be the one who was thrown out!
ND: Does anyone get it right when it comes to raising children?
Yes of course, you can't clump all children into one big basket. It's not unusual for older children here – teenagers of 14, 15 and 16 – to take out their little brothers and sisters for an evening stroll – they even seem happy for Grandma and Grandpa to come too.

I have a class of eight to ten year olds studying English with me and they're a pleasure to teach, very polite and respectful. We have a lot of fun and they learn a lot.

Caroline Sinfield, 35, language teacher, Alicante, Spain

My girlfriend loves kids, always has. Her job is helping younger kids with behavioural problems. When I told her I didn't want them there was an awkward silence but I felt it was the best way to go because I didn't want to get deep with someone and then have it all fall apart. Most women around here HAVE to have kids, there is no excuse not to and that is a fear for her. But she told me that she wanted to be with me and that she would stick with me.

She says that she likes to be able to come home to some peacefulness after working with kids all day. So in a way she still has kids and I still don't. I guess it works out for both of us.

I'm not sure if this has anything to do with my not wanting kids, but I had a pretty rough childhood. I was the centre of a custody battle when my parents split up. My mum snatched me and we were always on the run, trying to avoid being tracked down by the cops and the other half of my family. I can't count how many schools I was in. I think deep down I want to enjoy my life to make up for what was lost. Then maybe there is some fear in me that I don't want any kid of mine to go through that.

Since high school I was getting vibes that I was not really into having kids. I can remember when my nephew was born and how I felt when I held him for the first time. It was definitely a beautiful thing, but it was not something I felt comfortable with. I felt like I was holding an expensive vase. All I could think was, 'Don't drop this little guy.' When my sister-in-law was pregnant with their second baby, my niece, I had to keep making trips to a Mexican chain restaurant. She had those cravings pregnant women get. The whole thing seemed insane.

My oldest friend had a baby 2 years ago. If we hang out once a month for more than an hour it's a rarity these days. He always valued his alone time and I really feel for the guy. Now he works and he comes home and he works some more. He and his wife have to schedule 'dates' just to be together sometimes. They have a beautiful son and everything, but where is that sense of freedom to be able to come and go when you want?

Another thing I love about being childfree is having more money. Now I do not have the best job in the world, but I do okay. And it is such a great feeling to know that I have something extra put away for a rainy day or an unexpected bill. I still have my student loans to pay off and I can't even fathom trying to pay for childcare expenses on top of that.

I don't view anything about my decision as negative. Sometimes I wonder what it would be like to pass on things I have learned to someone, but then I am snapped back to reality by the time and energy that is needed for such a thing to happen. I could do it if I had the inclination, but I have nothing to prove to anyone. I have a wonderful girlfriend and I just want to be happy with her. If we're out at a restaurant and some kids are screaming we don't have to deal with it, we can go home and relax. Man that is a great feeling!

Mike, 30, shipping courier, Philadelphia, USA

Where I live, lots of girls get pregnant just as soon as they leave school. I don't have anybody who I can tell my feelings to, so I have written you an essay for your book.

This is where I stand: Colic, plastic toys and diaper bags do not interest me. Waiting for the school bus does not interest me. Parental permission forms, emergency room visits and middle school bullies do not interest me. Chaperoning proms does not interest me. Empty nest syndrome does not interest me. I am studying biology. I want to be a vet, a physician or a medical researcher.

In the beginning, I did dream of having children — four to be exact. Even though I am still only a teen, I had names picked out and everything. Then, when girls I'd grown up with began to get pregnant, I started to question how different life would be with and without children. I began to wonder if I wanted kids purely to gain the respect and status that society currently only gives to people who are doing 'the most important job in the world'. I pushed these thoughts to the back of my mind and believed that I would change my mind as I matured. Once we were on the school bus and the bus driver brought her screaming toddler along for the ride. 'I don't want any kids,' I blurted out to a friend seated beside me, and she replied, 'A baby is a gift from God,' looking at me with blank, self-righteous, sheep-like eyes. The Bible says that wine is a gift from God (I bet your Preacher never talks about this gift!) but you have to be a certain age before you can drink it and some people may even think it is better if I do not drink it!

I have thought about this subject a lot now. Unlike parenthood, a childfree decision is not made by leave-your-brain-at-the-door dogma or a broken condom. Childfree people have thought carefully about their decision in a way that would put most parents to shame. It's not easy because they are not supported everywhere by mindless slogans that support your group above all others. (Children are the Future! Kids go Free! For your Family and your Family's Family!) If parenthood is as important as society makes out, shouldn't it require more thought and common sense?

I don't dislike children, my dislike is reserved for the ignorant societies and the soccer mommies who can only see the value in people who share their genes ('he-has-Brad's-nose-and-my-blue-eyes'), drink out of juice boxes and say the 'darnedest things'. We have been conditioned by society to believe that motherhood is the be-all, end-all highest calling for women, but it reduces them. Women cannot have it all in this society no matter what the commercials say.

My mom's co-worker gave birth at 20, 21 and 23. My cousins have been procreating like cats since they were teens. Now they are in their twenties and have litters. A woman on the bus told me she had her first child at 20 and that 'was a good age'. No one

Afterword

This morning I got up early, intending to spend the day at my desk, but the day was one of those autumn jewels – cloudless, blue sky, a chill in the air and shallow warmth in the sun. I went to the gym and, rather than heading home as I should, was drawn to drift north to the Thames at Tower Bridge. I lay on my back on a concrete bench.

There were cargo ships on the river and the city was stirring to life, but every sound had a distant quality. I heard the Bow bells. I got my book from my bag and read a few chapters of *The Life of Pi*, which has absorbed me all week. I dozed a bit in the fresh air.

When I stirred and sat up, the sky seemed to have washed the city in white and blue and the sun was dazzling in the glass of the Swiss Re building. The day could be anything I wanted it to be. I felt drunkenly in love with life; a round peg in a round hole; comfortable in my own skin; utterly relaxed and happy.

Is this the feeling parents get when they look at their children sleeping? If it is, that's great – it's intoxicating.

If it's not, it's good enough for me.

References and Resources

Chapter 1 Freedom of Choice

1. UK Office for National Statistics (ONS), Census 2001; The Australian Bureau of Statistics; Statistics New Zealand; Statistics Canada; General Social Survey 2001 (Canada); Census of Japan
2. The Population Reference Bureau, www.prb.org
3. ONS Census 2001
4. *Will You Be Mother?: Women Who Choose To Say No* by Jane Bartlett, New York University Press, 1995
5. *Without Child: Challenging the Stigma of Childlessness* by Laurie Lisle, Routledge, 1999
6. *Childfree and Sterilized: Women's Decisions and Medical Responses* by Annily Campbell, Cassell, 1999

Chapter 3 Parent Propaganda

1. *Choosing Childlessness* by Fiona McAllister with Lynda Clarke, Family Policy Studies Centre, London, July 1998
2. *Family matters: Parents Living with Children in Old Age* by Judith Healey and Stella Yarrow, The Policy Press in association

with *Community Care* magazine and the Joseph Rowntree Foundation, UK; www.careguide.com (US)

3. *As Miss Nightingale Said* by Monica Baly, Medico Dental Media International, 1991

Chapter 4 Instinct and Reason

1. Survey of 1000 readers, *Good Housekeeping*, June 2003
2. *Instinct, A Study in Social Psychology* by Luther Lee Bernard, Henry Holt and Co, 1924
3. 'Life's more than just babies, says IVF chief', *Observer*, August 2002
4. *Choosing to be Different: Women, Work and The Family* by Jill Kirby, Centre for Policy Studies, London, June 2003; percentage figure taken from *Models of the Family in Modern Societies* by Catherine Hakim, Ashgate, 2004, p78, table 3.11
5. 'Time Trends in Adolescent Mental Health', *Journal of Child Psychology and Psychiatry*, November 2004. A 25-year study by the Institute of Psychiatry, King's College London and the University of Manchester.

Chapter 5 Consumerism

1. Survey by Carrick James Market Research for Axa Insurance UK. 250 adults and 250 children aged 8–16 responded to questionnaires in Manchester, Glasgow and Swansea, December 2003.
2. Survey by Mintel, April 2004
3. *Raising Responsive and Responsible Children* by Richard Gallagher PhD, Robin F Goodman PhD and Anita Gurian, PhD, New York University Child Study Centre
4. Child Poverty Action Group, UK; *Child Well-Being, Child Poverty and Child Policy in Modern Nations* by Koen Vleminckx and Timothy M Smeeding for the European Union, Policy Press, February 2001

5. 'Early Television Exposure and Subsequent Attention Problems in Children' by Dimitri A Christakis, *Pediatrics*, USA, April 2004
6. *Mother & Baby*, November 2003
7. 'Young Men Speak Out', by Young Voice for Samaritans, 1999, A Katz, A Buchanan and A McCoy, www.youngvoice.org, available free from The Samaritans
8. 'Deliberate Self Harm Among Children and Young People', *Updates*: Volume 4, Issue 16, The Mental Health Foundation, UK, May 2003
9. 'Youth Suicide in Australia', Australian Government, Department of Health and Ageing; '(Suicide) Statistics for Selected Countries', World Health Organisation

Chapter 6 Environment and Population

1. The Population Reference Bureau
2. David Willetts MP (Conservative), interview on *The Jeremy Vine Programme*, BBC Radio 2, September 2003
3. Policy Statement on Population, Family First Party, Australia
4. Stephen Hawking, interview on *Larry King Live Weekend*, CNN, December 1999
5. Global Competitiveness Report 2003-2004 by Professor Klaus Schwab, The World Economic Forum
6. 'UK Government Acts to Curb Rise in Tuberculosis', *British Medical Journal*: 329, 16 October 2004, p877; Henry Yeager Jr, MD, Professor of Medicine, Georgetown Medical Center, Washington, DC
7. 'China's One-Child Rule', http://geography.about.com
8. World Population Awareness, www.overpopulation.org; 'The World at Six Billion', United Nations Population Division
9. *Nightline*, ABC, January 17–18 2001

10. Speech to the Optimum Population Trust (OPT), David Attenborough, August 2003; *Sunday Times*, 3 August 2003
11. 'When Men Say Ladies First', *The Times of India*, December 2004
12. Optimum Population Trust (OPT), www.optimumpopulation.org
13. Professor Alan Trounson, The Monash Institute of Reproduction, Victoria, Australia; Allan Templeton, Royal College of Obstetricians and Gynaecologists, London; *The Guardian*, July 2003
14. Parents for Children, www.parentsforchildren.org.uk; WomenAid International Children of the World Initiative; Hope Worldwide www.hopeww.org (US)
15. 'Last Gasp' by Jonathan Porritt, BBC Open University, www.open2.net
16. 'Population Control: How Many Are Too Many?' by Morris Sullivan, *Impact*, www.impactpress.com
17. Friends of the Earth, www.foe.co.uk
18. 'Population Growth, Our Quality of Life and Environmental Sustainability', www.overpopulation.org
19. 'For Younger Latinas, A Shift to Smaller Families' *The New York Times*, December 2004
20. National Committee for a Human Life Amendment, www.nchla.org; Texans for Life Coalition, www.texlife.org
21. 'Women and Self Esteem' by Cara Swann, www.suite101.com
22. 'Schroder Adopts Russian Girl', World Press Reports, August 2004

Chapter 7 Work and Childcare

1. 'Women and Work', *Top Sante*/BUPA, June 2002
2. *In Praise of Slow* by Carl Honore, Cygnus Books, 2004
3. ONS, Census 2001

4. 'American Time Use Survey', US Department of Labor, Bureau of Labor Statistics
5. 'Early Childhood Education and Care Policy in Denmark', report for the OECD, Ministry of Social Affairs/Ministry of Education, Denmark , 2000
6. Local authority websites, www.lancashire.gov.uk/education, www.devon. gov.uk
7. 'Parents to Get Cash to Help Pay for Nannies', Children's Minister Margaret Hodge, Department for Education and Skills News Centre, UK, December 2004: 'The Government's ten year child care strategy is nothing short of a child care revolution'.
8. Women and Work Commission Interim Report 2005, 'Young Women No Longer Want It All', *Guardian*, March 2005
9. Young Women's Lifestyle Survey of Great Britain 2005, commissioned by *New Woman* magazine. 1500 women, average age 29, questioned.
10. Response to the Government Green Paper 'Work and Parents: Competitiveness and Choice' by Kidding Aside (The British Childfree Association), June 2001
11. Statistics compiled by Kidding Aside
12. Speech to Sure Start conference by Children's Minister Margaret Hodge, DfES News Centre, December 2004
13. The Clearinghouse on International Developments in Child, Youth and Family Policies, Columbia University, New York, www.childpolicyintl.org. See table 1: Child and Family Cash and Tax Benefits in Select Industrialized Countries.
14. DfES Childcare Approval Scheme, HM Treasury News Centre
15. Child Poverty Action Group, UK, www.cpag.org.uk; 'A League Table of Child Poverty in Rich Nations', UNICEF, June 2000

16. 'Universal Early Education and Care Promises Long Term Benefits for Britain', The Daycare Trust, UK
17. The Future Laboratory, London, www.thefuturelaboratory.com

Chapter 8 Men

1. Household, Income and Labour Dynamics Survey (HILDA), Australian Government, Department of Family and Community Services
2. Statistics Canada, General Social Survey 2001
3. 'Bringing Up Father' by Nancy Gibbs, cover story, *Time* magazine, June 1993
4. 'Spending Time With Dad', *Kearl's Guide to the Sociology of the Family: Parenting and Children,* Trinity University, San Antonio, Texas, www.trinity.edu
5. 'The Fate of Fathers Embroiled in Acrimonious Custody Battles Has Become Increasingly High Profile in Recent Months' by Sophie Blakemore, *Birmingham Post*, July 2004; 'Dads and Kids Stand to Lose Under New Law' by Ian Mulgrew, *Vancouver Sun*, April 2003
6. 'More Men Don't Want Children: Study' by Julie Szego, *The Age*, Melbourne, October 2002

Chapter 9 Sanctimonious Parents

1. 'Life After Birth' by Emily Wilson, *Guardian*, September 2004
2. 'Not the bike kids again ... they're crap' by Sarah Getty, *Metro*, July 2004

Chapter 10 Free Range Children

1. Preliminary figures from the Department of Education and Skills, www.educationguardian.co.uk, July 2004
2. 'Teens Believe They Learn to be Violent', study by

Children's Institute International, www.crf-usa.org/violence/alternative.html

3. 'Violent Behaviour Among Elementary and Middle School Children', *Journal of Pediatrics*, October 1999

Chapter 11 Honest Parents

1. '70% of Parents Say Kids Not Worth It', Ann Landers' Advice Column, syndicated US newspapers, 1975
2. Home-Start Parenting Survey 2000
3. 'The Lever Faberge Family Report 2003: Choosing Happiness?' by Kate Stanley, Laura Edwards and Becky Hatch/Institute of Public Policy Research
4. 'Battering and Pregnancy', *Midwifery Today* 1998; Women Health and Development Program, www.planetwire.org
5. 'Choosing to be Different: Women, Work and The Family' by Jill Kirby, Centre for Policy Studies, London, June 2003, p21
6. 'Couples in Pre-Kid, No-Kid Marriages Happiest', *USA Today*, 1997 (source: Mary Benin, Arizona State University for the American Sociological Association)

Chapter 12 What You Won't Be Missing Out On

1. 'Going Solo: Single Life in the 21st Century', BBC single life survey, February 2005
2. 'Couples Spend Just Two Hours Together a Day' by John Carvel, *Guardian*, July 2004; Time-Use Survey ONS, 2000
3. 'What Are You Really Arguing About' by Paula Hall, www.bbc.co.uk, February 2005; 'Couple Minutes: The Unsinkable Marriage', www.christianitytoday.com, 2001
4. 'Welcome to Grandparenthood', www.ageconcern.co.uk

The following books were of invaluable help in research:

What Are Children For? by Laurie Taylor and Matthew Taylor, Short Books, London, 2003
Why Is Sex Fun? The Evolution of Human Sexuality by Jared Diamond, Weidenfeld and Nicolson, London, 1997
The Mommy Myth: The Idealization of Motherhood and How it has Undermined Women by Susan J Douglas and Meredith W Michaels, Free Press, New York, 2004
The Population Explosion by Paul and Anne Ehrlich, Simon and Schuster, New York. 1990
Choosing Childlessness by Fiona McAllister with Lynda Clarke, Family Policy Studies Centre, London, 1998
Additional thanks to Hugh Small, author, *Florence Nightingale: Avenging Angel*, St Martin's Press, New York, 1998

Whether you want to make a political statement about being childfree, or just meet likeminded people, there's plenty of support around.

No Kidding! is the biggest online group. It was set up in Canada in 1984 and now has branches (they're called chapters) all over the world. It's a non-political, international social club that brings people together in person as well as via the internet: www.nokidding.net.

The World Childfree Association is based in Australia and has aspirations to become a political party. It raises the awareness of choice surrounding parenthood and promotes a childfree way of life as a valid way of life: www.worldchildfree.org.

In the UK, Kidding Aside describes itself as a grassroots political organisation calling for equal rights for parents and childfree people: www.kiddingaside.net.

Parentline Plus, mentioned earlier in the book, run a free 24 hour Advice Line in the UK: 0808 800 2222.

Acknowledgements

Thank you to everyone who contributed to the research for this book, from so many countries, in any way shape or form. The response was not only fantastic in quantity but in the quality of inspiring stories.

Thanks also to Sam Adams, James Armoogum, Emily Bird, Louise Coe, Charlotte Cole, Alex Dalton, Julie Defago, Sheena Dewan, Neil and Helen Humphrey, Olly Keen, David Lumsden, Simon Mann, Juliet Nicolson, Jeremy Paxman, Helen Persighetti, Liz Puttick, Paul Swallow, Rowena Webster and Laura Yule.

To Parentline Plus for making me welcome, staff and regulars at SoBo, Tower Bridge Road who joined in the debate over the best coffee in town, and to Jim.

About the Author

Nicki Defago is a journalist. She worked as a senior producer at the BBC's *Newsnight* and was Deputy Editor of *The Jeremy Vine Programme* on Radio 2. Her print articles have appeared in *Red*, *She* and *Eve* magazines. Nicki was born in 1966, is married and lives in London.